T0185419

Practical Spring LDAP

Enterprise Java LDAP Development Made Easy

Balaji Varanasi

Apress·

Practical Spring LDAP: Enterprise Java LDAP Development Made Easy

Copyright © 2013 Balaji Varanasi. All rights reserved.

This work is subject to copyright. All rights are reserved by the Publisher, whether the whole or part of the material is concerned, specifically the rights of translation, reprinting, reuse of illustrations, recitation, broadcasting, reproduction on microfilms or in any other physical way, and transmission or information storage and retrieval, electronic adaptation, computer software, or by similar or dissimilar methodology now known or hereafter developed. Exempted from this legal reservation are brief excerpts in connection with reviews or scholarly analysis or material supplied specifically for the purpose of being entered and executed on a computer system, for exclusive use by the purchaser of the work. Duplication of this publication or parts thereof is permitted only under the provisions of the Copyright Law of the Publisher's location, in its current version, and permission for use must always be obtained from Springer. Permissions for use may be obtained through RightsLink at the Copyright Clearance Center. Violations are liable to prosecution under the respective Copyright Law.

ISBN-13 (pbk): 978-1-4302-6397-5

ISBN-13 (electronic): 978-1-4302-6398-2

Trademarked names, logos, and images may appear in this book. Rather than use a trademark symbol with every occurrence of a trademarked name, logo, or image we use the names, logos, and images only in an editorial fashion and to the benefit of the trademark owner, with no intention of infringement of the trademark.

The use in this publication of trade names, trademarks, service marks, and similar terms, even if they are not identified as such, is not to be taken as an expression of opinion as to whether or not they are subject to proprietary rights.

While the advice and information in this book are believed to be true and accurate at the date of publication, neither the authors nor the editors nor the publisher can accept any legal responsibility for any errors or omissions that may be made. The publisher makes no warranty, express or implied, with respect to the material contained herein.

President and Publisher: Paul Manning
Lead Editor: Steve Anglin
Development Editor: Tom Welsh
Technical Reviewer: Manual Jordan
Editorial Board: Steve Anglin, Mark Beckner, Ewan Buckingham, Gary Cornell, Louise Corrigan, Morgan Ertel, Jonathan Gennick, Jonathan Hassell, Robert Hutchinson, Michelle Lowman, James Markham, Matthew Moodie, Jeff Olson, Jeffrey Pepper, Douglas Pundick, Ben Renow-Clarke, Dominic Shakeshaft, Gwenan Spearing, Matt Wade, Tom Welsh
Coordinating Editor: Anamika Panchoo
Copy Editor: Mary Behr
Compositor: SPi Global
Indexer: SPi Global
Artist: SPi Global
Cover Designer: Anna Ishchenko

Distributed to the book trade worldwide by Springer Science+Business Media New York, 233 Spring Street, 6th Floor, New York, NY 10013. Phone 1-800-SPRINGER, fax (201) 348-4505, e-mail orders-ny@springer-sbm.com, or visit www.springeronline.com. Apress Media, LLC is a California LLC and the sole member (owner) is Springer Science + Business Media Finance Inc (SSBM Finance Inc). SSBM Finance Inc is a **Delaware** corporation.

For information on translations, please e-mail rights@apress.com, or visit www.apress.com.

Apress and friends of ED books may be purchased in bulk for academic, corporate, or promotional use. eBook versions and licenses are also available for most titles. For more information, reference our Special Bulk Sales–eBook Licensing web page at www.apress.com/bulk-sales.

Any source code or other supplementary materials referenced by the author in this text is available to readers at www.apress.com. For detailed information about how to locate your book's source code, go to www.apress.com/source-code/.

To my life, Sudha

Contents at a Glance

Contents

About the Author

Balaji Varanasi is a software development manager and technology entrepreneur. He has over 13 years of experience architecting and developing Java/.NET applications and, more recently, iPhone apps. During this period he has worked in the areas of security, web accessibility, search, and enterprise portals. He has a Master's Degree in Computer Science and serves as faculty, teaching programming and information system courses. He shares his insights and experiments at `http://blog.inflinx.com`. When not programming, he enjoys spending time with his lovely wife in Salt Lake City, Utah.

About the Technical Reviewer

Manuel Jordan Elera is an autodidactic developer and researcher who enjoys learning new technologies for his own experiments and creating new integrations.

Manuel won the 2010 Springy Award – Community Champion and Spring Champion 2013. In his little free time, he reads the Bible and composes music on his guitar. Manuel is a Senior Member in the **Spring Community Forums**, known as dr_pompeii.

Manuel has acted as Technical Reviewer for these books (all published by Apress):

Pro SpringSource dm Server (2009)

Spring Enterprise Recipes (2009)

Spring Recipes (Second Edition) (2010)

Pro Spring Integration (2011)

Pro Spring Batch (2011)

Pro Spring 3 (2012)

Pro Spring MVC: With Web Flow (2012)

Pro Spring Security (2013)

Pro Hibernate and MongoDB (2013)

Pro JPA 2 (Second Edition) (2013)

Read and contact him through his blog at http://manueljordan.wordpress.com/ and follow him on his Twitter account, @dr_pompeii.

Acknowledgements

This book would not have been possible without the support of several people, and I would like to take this opportunity to sincerely thank them.

Thanks to the amazing people at Apress: most importantly, Steve Anglin, Tom Welsh, Anamika Panchoo, Mary Behr, and many others. Many thanks to Manuel Jordan Elera for his technical review and the valuable feedback he provided.

Special thanks to my friends Mike Mormando and Steve Trousdale. Your suggestions helped me refine and improve this book's content.

Finally, I would like to thank my wife for her constant support and encouragement in all my endeavors. Without you, this book would not have been possible.

—Balaji

Introduction

Practical Spring LDAP provides a complete coverage of Spring LDAP, a framework designed to take the pain out of LDAP programming. This book starts by explaining the fundamental concepts of LDAP and showing the reader how to set up the development environment. It then dives into Spring LDAP, analyzing the problems it is designed to solve. After that, the book focuses on the practical aspects of unit testing and integration testing LDAP code. This is followed by an in-depth treatment of LDAP controls and new Spring LDAP 1.3.1 features such as Object Directory Mapping and LDIF parsing. Finally, it concludes with discussions of LDAP authentication and connection pooling.

What the Book Covers

Chapter 1 starts with an overview of directory servers. It then discusses basics of LDAP and introduces the four LDAP information models. It finishes up with an introduction to the LDIF format that is used for representing LDAP data.

Chapter 2 focuses on the Java Naming and Directory Interface (JNDI). In this chapter, you look at creating applications that interact with LDAP using plain JNDI.

Chapter 3 explains what Spring LDAP is and why it is an important option in an enterprise developer's repertoire. In this chapter, you set up the development environment needed to create Spring LDAP applications, and other important tools such as Maven and a test LDAP server. Finally, you implement a basic but complete Spring LDAP application using annotations.

Chapter 4 covers the fundamentals of Unit/Mock/Integration testing. You then look at setting up an embedded LDAP server for unit testing your application code. You also review available tools for generating test data. Finally, you use EasyMock framework to mock test LDAP code.

Chapter 5 introduces the basics of JNDI object factories and using these factories for creating objects that are more meaningful to the application. You then examine a complete Data Access Object (DAO) layer implementation using Spring LDAP and object factories.

Chapter 6 covers LDAP Search. This chapter begins with the underlying ideas of LDAP Search. I then introduce various Spring LDAP Filters that make LDAP searching easier. Finally, you look at creating a custom search filter to address situations where the current set is not sufficient.

Chapter 7 provides an in-depth overview of LDAP controls that can be used for extending LDAP server functionality. Then it moves on to sorting and paging LDAP results using sort and page controls.

Chapter 8 deals with Object-Directory Mapping, a new feature that was introduced in Spring LDAP 1.3.1. In this chapter, you look at bridging the gap between domain model and directory server. You then re-implement the DAO using ODM concepts.

Chapter 9 introduces the important ideas of transactions and transactional integrity, before analyzing the transaction abstractions provided by Spring Framework. Finally, it takes a look at Spring LDAP's compensating transaction support.

Chapter 10 starts with implementing authentication, the most common operation performed against LDAP. It then deals with parsing LDIF files using another feature that was introduced in Spring 1.3.1. I end the chapter by looking at the connection pooling support provided by Spring LDAP.

Target Audience

Practical Spring LDAP is intended for developers interested in building Java/JEE applications using LDAP. It also teaches techniques for creating unit/integration tests for LDAP applications. The book assumes basic familiarity with Spring Framework; prior exposure to LDAP is helpful but not required. Developers who are already familiar with Spring LDAP will find best practices and examples that can help them get the most out of the framework.

Downloading Source Code

The source code for the examples in this book can be downloaded from `www.apress.com`. For detailed information about how to locate this book's source code, go to `www.apress.com/source-code/`. The code is organized by chapter and can be built using Maven.

The code uses Spring LDAP 1.3.2 and Spring Framework 3.2.4. It is tested against OpenDJ and ApacheDS LDAP servers. More information on getting started can be found in Chapter 3.

Questions?

If you have any questions or suggestions, you can contact the author at `balaji@inflinx.com`.

CHAPTER 1

■ ■ ■

Introduction to LDAP

In this chapter, we will discuss:

- Directory basics
- LDAP information models
- LDIF format for representing LDAP data
- A sample application

We all deal with directories on a daily basis. We use a telephone directory to look up phone numbers. When visiting a library, we use the library catalog to look up the books we want to read. With computers, we use the file system directory to store our files and documents. Simply put, a directory is a repository of information. The information is usually organized in such a way that it can be retrieved easily.

Directories on a network are typically accessed using the client/server communication model. Applications wanting to read or write data to a directory communicate with specialized directory servers. The directory server performs read or write operation on the actual directory. Figure 1-1 shows this client/server interaction.

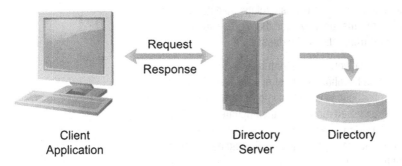

Figure 1-1. *Directory server and client interaction*

The communication between the directory server and client applications is usually accomplished using standardized protocols. The Lightweight Directory Access Protocol (LDAP) provides a standard protocol model for communicating with a directory. The directory servers that implement the LDAP protocol are usually referred to as LDAP servers. The LDAP protocol is based on an earlier X.500 standard but is significantly simpler (and hence lightweight) and easily extensible. Over the years, the LDAP protocol went through iterations and is currently at version 3.0.

LDAP Overview

The LDAP defines a message protocol used by directory clients and directory servers. LDAP can be better understood by considering the following four models upon which it is based:

- The Information model determines the structure of information stored in the directory.

- The Naming model defines how information is organized and identified in the directory.

- The Functional model defines the operations that can be performed on the directory.

- The Security model defines how to protect information from unauthorized access.

We will be looking at each of these models in the sections that follow.

DIRECTORY VS. DATABASE

Beginners often get confused and picture an LDAP directory as a relational database. Like a database, an LDAP directory stores information. However, there are several key characteristics that set a directory apart from relational databases.

LDAP directories typically store data that is relatively static in nature. For example, employee information stored in LDAP such as his phone number or name does not change every day. However, users and applications look up this information very frequently. Since the data in a directory is accessed more often than updated, LDAP directories follow the WORM principle (http://en.wikipedia.org/wiki/Write_Once_Read_Many) and are heavily optimized for read performance. Placing data that change quite often in an LDAP does not make sense.

Relational databases employ techniques such as referential integrity and locking to ensure data consistency. The type of data stored in LDAP usually does not warrant such strict consistency requirements. Hence, most of these features are absent on LDAP servers. Also, transactional semantics to roll back transactions are not defined under LDAP specification.

Relational databases are designed following normalization principles to avoid data duplication and data redundancy. LDAP directories, on the other hand, are organized in a hierarchical, object-oriented way. This organization violates some of the normalization principles. Also, there is no concept of table joins in LDAP.

Even though directories lack several of the RDBMS features mentioned above, many modern LDAP directories are built on top of relational databases such as DB2.

Information Model

The basic unit of information stored in LDAP is referred to as an entry. Entries hold information about real world objects such as employees, servers, printers, and organizations. Each entry in an LDAP directory is made up of zero or more attributes. Attributes are simply key value pairs that hold information about the object represented by the entry. The key portion of an attribute is also called the attribute type and describes the kind of information that can be stored in the attribute. The value portion of the attribute contains the actual information. Table 1-1 shows a portion of an entry representing an employee. The left column in the entry contains the attribute types, and the right column holds the attribute values.

Table 1-1. *Employee LDAP Entry*

Employee Entry	
objectClass	inetOrgPerson
givenName	John
surname	Smith
mail	john@inflix.com
	jsmith@inflix.com
mobile	+1 801 100 1000

■ **Note**   Attribute names by default are case-insensitive. However, it is recommended to use camel case format in LDAP operations.

You will notice that the mail attribute has two values. Attributes that are allowed to hold multiple values are called multi-valued attributes. Single-valued attributes, on the other hand, can only hold a single value. The LDAP specification does not guarantee the order of the values in a multi-valued attribute.

Each attribute type is associated with a syntax that dictates the format of the data stored as attribute value. For example, the mobile attribute type has a TelephoneNumber syntax associated with it. This forces the attribute to hold a string value with length between 1 and 32. Additionally, the syntax also defines the attribute value behavior during search operations. For example, the givenName attribute has the syntax DirectoryString. This syntax enforces that only alphanumeric characters are allowed as values. Table 1-2 lists some of the common attributes along with their associated syntax description.

Table 1-2. *Common Entry Attributes*

Attribute Type	Syntax	Description
commonName	DirectoryString	Stores the common name of a person.
telephoneNumber	TelephoneNumber	Stores the person's primary telephone number.
jpegPhoto	Binary	Stores one or more images of the person.
Surname	DirectoryString	Stores the last name of the person.
employeeNumber	DirectoryString	Stores the employee's identification number in the organization.
givenName	DirectoryString	Stores user's first name.
mail	IA5 String	Stores person's SMTP mail address.
mobile	TelephoneNumber	Stores person's mobile number.
postalAddress	Postal Address	Stores the location of the user.
postalCode	DirectoryString	Stores the user's ZIP or postal code.
st	DirectoryString	Stores the state or province name.
uid	DirectoryString	Stores the user id.
street	DirectoryString	Stores the street address.

Object Classes

In object-oriented languages such as Java, we create a class and use it as a blueprint for creating objects. The class defines the attributes/data (and behavior/methods) that these instances can have. In a similar fashion, object classes in LDAP determine the attributes an LDAP entry can have. These object classes also define which of these attributes are mandatory and which are optional. Every LDAP entry has a special attribute aptly named objectClass that holds the object class it belongs to. Looking at the objectClass value in the employee entry in Table 1-1, we can conclude that the entry belongs to the inetOrgPerson class. Table 1-3 shows the required and optional attributes in a standard LDAP person object class. The cn attribute holds the person's common name whereas the sn attribute holds the person's family name or surname.

Table 1-3. *Person Object Class*

Required Attributes	Optional Attributes
sn	description
	telephoneNumber
cn	userPassword
objectClass	seeAlso

As in Java, it is possible for an object class to extend other object classes. This inheritance will allow the child object class to inherit parent class attributes. For example, the person object class defines attributes such as common name and surname. The object class inetOrgPerson extends the person class and thus inherits all the person's attributes. Additionally, inetOrgPerson defines attributes that are required for a person working in an organization, such as departmentNumber and employeeNumber. One special object class namely top does not have any parents. All other object classes are decedents of top and inherit all the attributes declared in it. The top object class includes the mandatory objectClass attribute. Figure 1-2 shows the object inheritance.

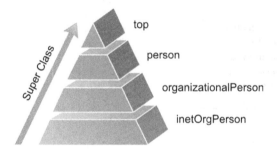

Figure 1-2. *LDAP object inheritance*

Most LDAP implementations come with a set of standard object classes that can be used out of the box. Table 1-4 lists some of these LDAP object classes along with their commonly used attributes.

Table 1-4. *Common LDAP Object Classes*

Object Class	Attributes	Description
top	objectClass	Defines the root object class. All other object classes must extend this class.
organization	o	Represents a company or an organization. The o attribute typically holds the name of the organization.
organizationalUnit	ou	Represents a department or similar entity inside an organization.
person	sn cn telephoneNumber userPassword	Represents a person in the directory and requires the sn (surname) and cn (common name) attributes.
organizationalPerson	registeredAddress postalAddress postalCode	Subclasses person and represents a person in an organization.
inetOrgPerson	uid departmentNumber employeeNumber givenName manager	Provides additional attributes and can be used to represent a person working in today's Internet- and intranet-based organization. The uid attribute holds the person's username or user id.

Directory Schema

The LDAP directory schema is a set of rules that determine the type of information stored in a directory. Schemas can be considered as packaging units and contain attribute type definitions and object class definitions. Before an entry can be stored in LDAP, the schema rules are verified. This schema checking ensures that the entry has all the required attributes and does not contain any attributes that are not part of the schema. Figure 1-3 represents a generic LDAP schema.

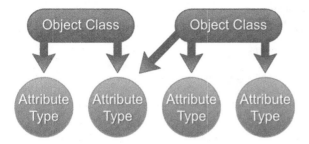

Figure 1-3. *LDAP generic schema*

Like databases, directory schemas need to be well designed to address issues like data redundancy. Before you go about implementing your own schema, it is worth looking at several of the standard schemas available publicly. Most often these standard schemas contain all definitions to store the required data and, more importantly, ensure interoperability across other directories.

Naming Model

The LDAP Naming model defines how entries are organized in a directory. It also determines how a particular entry can be uniquely identified. The Naming model recommends that entries be stored logically in a hierarchical fashion. This tree of entries is often referred to as directory information tree (DIT). Figure 1-4 provides an example of a generic directory tree.

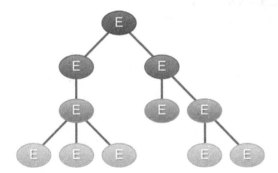

Figure 1-4. *Generic DIT*

The root of the tree is usually referred to as the base or suffix of the directory. This entry represents the organization that owns the directory. The format of suffix can vary from implementation to implementation but, in general, there are three recommended approaches, as listed in Figure 1-5.

7

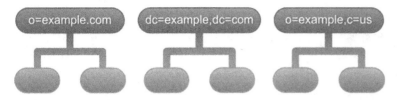

Figure 1-5. *Directory suffix naming conventions*

■ **Note**   DC stands for domain component.

The first recommended technique is to use the organization's do- main name as the suffix. For example, if the organization's domain name is example.com, the suffix of the directory will be o=example. com. The second technique also uses the domain name but each component of the name is prepended with "dc=" and joined by commas. So the domain name example.com would result in a suffix dc=example, dc=com. This technique is proposed in RFC 2247 and is popular with Microsoft Active Directory. The third technique uses X.500 model and creates a suffix in the format o=organization name, c=country code. In United States, the suffix for the organization example would be o=example, c=us.

The Naming model also defines how to uniquely name and identify entries in a directory. Entries that share a common immediate parent are uniquely identified via their Relative Distinguished Name (RDN). The RDN is computed using one or more attribute/value pairs of the entry. In its simplest case, RDN is usually of the form attribute name = attribute value. Figure 1-6 provides a simplified representation of an organization directory. Each person entry under ou=employees has a unique uid. So the RDN for the first person entry would be uid=emp1, where emp1 is the employee's user id.

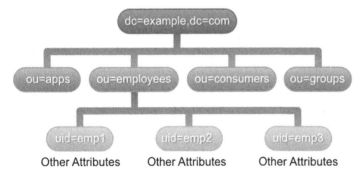

Figure 1-6. *Example of an organization directory*

> ■ **Note** The distinguished name is not an actual attribute in the entry. It is simply a logical name associated with the entry.

It is important to remember that RDN cannot be used to uniquely identify the entry in the entire tree. However, this can be easily done by combining the RDNs of all the entries in the path from the top of the tree to the entry. The result of this combination is referred to as Distinguished Name (DN). In Figure 1-6, the DN for Person 1 would be uid=emp1, ou=employees, dc=example, dc=com. Since the DN is made by combining RDNs, if an entry's RDN changes, the DNs of that entry and all its child entries also changes.

There can be situations where a set of entries do not have a single unique attribute. In those scenarios, one option is to combine multiple attributes to create uniqueness. For example, in the previous directory we can use the consumer's common name and e-mail address as a RDN. Multi-valued RDNs are represented by separating each attribute pair with a +, like so:

```
cn = Balaji Varanasi + mail=balaji@inflinx.com
```

> ■ **Note** Multi-valued RDNs are usually discouraged. In those scenarios, it is recommended to create a unique sequence attribute to ensure uniqueness.

Functional Model

The LDAP Functional model describes the access and modification operations that can be performed on the directory using LDAP protocol. These operations fall in to three categories: query, update, and authentication.

The query operations are used to search and retrieve information from a directory. So every time some information needs to be read, a search query needs to be constructed and executed against LDAP. The search operation takes a starting point within DIT, the depth of the search, and the attributes an entry must have for a match. In Chapter 6, you'll delve deep into searching and look at all the available options.

The update operations add, modify, delete, and rename directory entries. The add operation, as name suggests, adds a new entry to the directory. This operation requires the DN of the entry to be created and a set of attributes that constitute the entry. The delete operation takes a fully qualified DN of the entry and deletes it from the directory. The LDAP protocol allows only the leaf entries to be deleted. The modify operation updates an existing entry. This operation takes the entry's DN and a set of modifications such as adding a new attribute, updating a new attribute, or removing an existing attribute. The rename operation can be used to rename or move entries in a directory.

The authentication operations are used for connecting and ending sessions between the client and LDAP server. A bind operation initiates an LDAP session between the client and LDAP server. Typically, this would result in an anonymous session. It is possible for the client to provide a DN and set of credentials to authenticate itself and create an authenticated session. The unbind operation, on the other hand, can be used to terminate existing session and disconnect from the server.

LDAP V3 introduced a framework for extending existing operations and adding new operations without changing the protocol itself. You will take a look at these operations in Chapter 7.

Security Model

The LDAP Security model focuses on protecting LDAP directory information from unauthorized accesses. The model specifies which clients can access which parts of the directory and what kinds of operations (search vs. update) are allowed.

The LDAP Security model is based on the client authenticating itself to the server. This authentication process or bind operation as discussed above involves the client supplying a DN identifying itself and a password. If the client does not provide DN and password, an anonymous session is established. RFC 2829 (www.ietf.org/rfc/rfc2829.txt) defines a set of authentication methods that LDAP V3 servers must support. After successful authentication, the access control models are consulted to determine whether the client has sufficient privileges to do what is being requested. Unfortunately, no standards exist when it comes to access control models and each vendor provides his own implementations.

LDAP Vendors

LDAP has gained a wide support from a variety of vendors. There has also been a strong open source movement to produce LDAP servers. Table 1-5 outlines some of the popular Directory Servers.

Table 1-5. *LDAP Vendors*

Directory Name	Vendor	Open Source?	URL
Apache DS	Apache	Yes	http://directory.apache.org/apacheds/
OpenLDAP	OpenLDAP	Yes	www.openldap.org/
OpenDS	Oracle (formerly Sun)	Yes	hwww.opends.org/
Tivoli Directory Server	IBM	No	www.ibm.com/software/tivoli/products/directory-server

(continued)

Table 1-5. (*continued*)

Directory Name	Vendor	Open Source?	URL

Active Directory	Microsoft	No	`http://msdn.microsoft.com/`
			`en-us/library/windows/desktop/`
			`aa746492(v=vs.85).aspx`

eDirectory	Novell	No	`www.novell.com/` `products/edirectory/`

Oracle Directory Server Enterprise Edition	Oracle (formerly Sun)	No	`www.oracle.com/technetwork/`
			`middleware/id-mgmt/overview/`
			`index-085178.html`

Internet Directory	Oracle	No	`www.oracle.com/technetwork/`
			`middleware/id-mgmt/overview/`
			`index-082035.html`

OpenDJ	ForgeRock Community	Yes	`http://opendj.forgerock.org/`

ApacheDS and OpenDJ are pure Java implementation of LDAP directories. You will be using these two servers for unit and integration testing of the code throughout this book.

LDIF Format

The LDAP Data Interchange Format (LDIF) is a standard text-based format for representing directory content and update requests. The LDIF format is defined in RFC 2849 (`www.ietf.org/rfc/rfc2849.txt`). LDIF files are typically used to export data from one directory server and import it into another directory server. It is also popular for archiving directory data and applying bulk updates to a directory. You will be using LDIF files to store your test data and refreshing directory server between unit tests.

The basic format of an entry represented in LDIF is as follows:

```
#comment
dn: <distinguished name>
objectClass:  <object class>
objectClass:  <object class>
...
...
<attribute  type>: <attribute  value>
<attribute  type>: <attribute  value>
...
```

Lines in the LDIF file starting with a # character are considered as comments. The dn and at least one objectClass definition of the entry are considered required. Attributes are represented as name/value pairs separated by a colon. Multiple attribute values are specified in separate lines and will have the same attribute type. Since LDIF files are purely text-based, binary data needs to be Base64 encoded before it is stored as part of the LDIF file.

Multiple entries in the same LDIF file are separated by blank lines. Listing 1-1 shows an LDIF file with three employee entries. Notice that the cn attribute is a multivalued attribute and is represented twice for each employee.

Listing 1-1. LDIF File with Three Employee Entries

```
#  Barbara's Entry
dn: cn=Barbara J Jensen,  dc=example, dc=com
#  multi valued attribute
cn: Barbara J Jensen
cn:  Babs Jensen
objectClass:  person
sn: Jensen

#  Bjorn's  Entry
dn: cn=Bjorn J Jensen,  dc=example, dc=com
cn: Bjorn J Jensen
cn:  Bjorn Jensen
objectClass:  person
sn: Jensen
#  Base64 encoded  JPEG  photo
jpegPhoto:: /9j/4AAQSkZJRgABAAAAAQABAAD/2wBDABALD
A4MChAODQ4SERATGCgaGBYWGDEjJROoOjM9PDkzODdASFxOQ ERXRTc4UG1RV19iZ2hnPk1xeXBk
eFxlZ2P/2wBDARESEhgVG

#  Jennifer's  Entry
dn: cn=Jennifer  J Jensen,  dc=example, dc=com
cn: Jennifer J Jensen
cn: Jennifer  Jensen
objectClass: person
sn: Jensen
```

Sample Application

Throughout this book you will be working with a directory for a hypothetical book library. I have chosen library because the concept is universal and easy to grasp. A library usually stores books and other multimedia that patrons can borrow. Libraries also employs people for taking care of daily library operations. To keep things manageable, the directory will not be storing information about books. A relational database is probably suitable for recording book information. Figure 1-7 shows the LDAP directory tree for our library application.

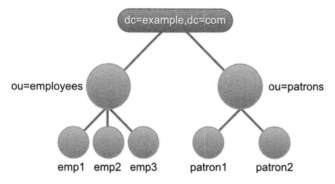

Figure 1-7. *Library DIT*

In this directory tree I have used the RFC 2247 (`www.ietf.org/rfc/rfc2247.txt`) convention for naming the base entry. The base entry has two organizational unit entries that hold the employees and patrons information. The ou=employees part of the tree will hold all the library employee entries. The ou=patrons part of the tree will hold the library patron entries. Both library employee and patron entries are of the type `inetOrgPerson` `objectClass`. Both employees and patrons access library applications using their unique login id. Thus the `uid` attribute will be used as the RDN for entries.

Summary

LDAP and applications that interact with LDAP have become a key part of every enterprise today. This chapter covered the basics of LDAP Directory. You learned that LDAP stores information as entries. Each entry is made up of attributes that are simply key value pairs. These entries can be accessed via their Distinguished Names. You also saw that LDAP directories have schemas that determine the type of information that can be stored.

In the next chapter, you will look at communicating with an LDAP directory using JNDI. In the chapters following Chapter 2, you will focus on using Spring LDAP for developing LDAP applications.

CHAPTER 2

■ ■ ■

Java Support for LDAP

In this chapter, we will discuss:

> » Basics of JNDI
>
> » LDAP enabling applications using JNDI
>
> » JNDI drawbacks

The Java Naming and Directory Interface (JNDI), as the name suggests provides a standardized programming interface for accessing naming and directory services. It is a generic API and can be used to access a variety of systems including file systems, EJB, CORBA, and directory services such as Network Information Service and LDAP. JNDI's abstractions to directory services can be viewed as similar to JDBC's abstractions to relational databases.

The JNDI architecture consists of an Application Programming Interface or API and a Service Provider Interface or SPI. Developers program their Java applications using the JNDI API to access directory/naming services. Vendors implement the SPI with details that deal with actual communication to their particular service/product. Such implementations are referred to as service providers. Figure 2-1 shows the JNDI architecture along with a few naming and directory service providers. This pluggable architecture provides a consistent programming model and prevents the need to learn a separate API for each product.

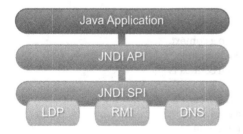

Figure 2-1. *JNDI Architecture*

The JNDI has been part of the standard JDK distribution since Java version 1.3. The API itself is spread across the following four packages:

» javax.naming package contains classes and interfaces for looking up and accessing objects in a naming service.

» javax.naming.directory package contains classes and interfaces that extend the core javax.naming package. These classes can be used to access directory services and perform advanced operations such as filtered searching.

» javax.naming.event package has functionality for event notification when accessing naming and directory services.

» javax.naming.ldap package contains classes and interfaces that support the LDAP Version 3 controls and operations. We will be looking at controls and operations in the later chapters.

The javax.naming.spi package contains the SPI interfaces and classes. Like I mentioned above, service providers implement SPI and we will not be covering these classes in this book.

LDAP Using JNDI

While JNDI allows access to a directory service, it is important to remember that JNDI itself is not a directory or a naming service. Thus, in order to access LDAP using JNDI, we need a running LDAP directory server. If you don't have a test LDAP server available, please refer to steps in Chapter 3 for installing a local LDAP server.

Accessing LDAP using JNDI usually involves the following three steps:

» Connect to LDAP

» Perform LDAP operations

» Close the resources

Connecting to LDAP

All the naming and directory operations using JNDI are performed relative to a context. So the first step in using JNDI is to create a context that acts as a starting point on the LDAP server. Such a context is referred to as an initial context. Once an initial context is established, it can be used to look up other contexts or add new objects.

The Context interface and InitialContext class in the javax.naming package can be used for creating an initial naming context. Since we are dealing with a directory here, we will be using a more specific DirContext interface and its implementation InitialDirContext. Both DirContext and InitialDirContext are available inside the javax. naming.directory package. The directory context instances can be configured with a set of properties that provide information about the LDAP server. The following code in Listing 2-1 creates a context to an LDAP server running locally on port 11389.

Listing 2-1.

```
Properties environment =  new  Properties();
environment.setProperty(DirContext.INITIAL_CONTEXT_FACTORY,
"com.sun.jndi.ldap.LdapCtxFactory");
environment.setProperty(DirContext.PROVIDER_URL, "ldap://localhost:11389");
DirContext context  =  new  InitialDirContext(environment);
```

In the above code, we have used the INITIAL_CONTEXT_FACTORY constant to specify the service provider class that needs to be used. Here we are using the sun provider com.sun.jndi.ldap.LdapCtxFactory, which is part of the standard JDK distribution. The PROVIDER_URL is used to specify the fully qualified URL of the LDAP server. The URL includes the protocol (ldap for non secure or ldaps for secure connections), the LDAP server host name and the port.

Once a connection to the LDAP server is established it is possible for the application to identify itself by providing authentication information. Contexts like the one created in Listing 2-1, where authentication information is not provided are referred to as anonymous contexts. LDAP servers usually have ACLs (access list controls) in place that restrict operations and information to certain accounts. So it is very common in enterprise applications to create and use authenticated contexts. Listing 2-2 provides an example of creating an authenticated context. Notice that we have used three additional properties to provide the binding credentials. The SECURITY_AUTHENTICATION property is set to simple indicating that we will be using plain text user name and password for authentication.

Listing 2-2.

```
Properties environment =  new  Properties();
environment.setProperty(DirContext.INITIAL_CONTEXT_FACTORY,
"com.sun.jndi.ldap.LdapCtxFactory");
environment.setProperty(DirContext.PROVIDER_URL, "ldap://localhost:11389");
environment.setProperty(DirContext.SECURITY_AUTHENTICATION, "simple");
environment.setProperty(DirContext.SECURITY_PRINCIPAL, "uid=admin,ou=system");
environment.setProperty(DirContext.SECURITY_CREDENTIALS, "secret");
DirContext context  =  new  InitialDirContext(environment);
```

Any problems that might occur during the creation of the context will be reported as instances of javax.naming.NamingException. NamingException is the super class of all the exceptions thrown by the JNDI API. This is a checked exception and must be handled properly for the code to compile. Table 2-1 provides a list of common exceptions that we are likely to encounter during JNDI development.

Table 2-1. *Common LDAP Exceptions*

Exception	Description
AttributeInUseException	Thrown when an operation tries to add an existing attribute.
AttributeModification Exception	Thrown when an operation tries to add/remove/ update an attribute and violates the attribute's schema or state. For example, adding two values to a single valued attribute would result in this exception.
CommunicationException	Thrown when an application fails to communicate (network problems for example) with the LDAP server.
InvalidAttributesException	Thrown when an operation tries to add or modify an attribute set that has been specified incompletely or incorrectly. For example, attempting to add a new entry without specifying all the required attributes would result in this exception.
LimitExceededException	Thrown when a search operation abruptly terminates as a user or system specified result limit is reached.
InvalidSearchFilterException	Thrown when a search operation is given a malformed search filter.
NameAlreadyBoundException	Thrown to indicate that an entry cannot be added as the associated name is already bound to a different object.
PartialResultException	Thrown to indicate that only a portion of the expected results is returned and the operation cannot be completed.

LDAP Operations

Once we obtain an initial context, we can perform a variety of operations on LDAP using the context. These operations can involve looking up another context, creating a new context and updating or removing an existing context. Here is an example of looking up another context with DN uid=emp1,ou=employees,dc=inflinx,d c=com.

```
DirContext anotherContext  =  context.lookup("uid=emp1,ou=employees,
dc=inflinx,dc=com");
```

We will take a closer look at each of these operations in the coming section.

Closing Resources

After all the desired LDAP operations are complete, it is important to properly close the context and any other associated resources. Closing a JNDI resource simply involves calling the close method on it. Listing 2-3 shows the code associated with closing a DirContext. From the code you can see that the close method also throws a NamingException that needs to be properly handled.

Listing 2-3.

```
try {
    context.close();
}
catch (NamingException e) {
    e.printstacktrace();
}
```

Creating a New Entry

Consider the case where a new employee starts with our hypothetical Library and we are asked to add his information to LDAP. As we have seen earlier, before an entry can be added to LDAP, it is necessary to obtain an InitialDirContext. Listing 2-4 defines a reusable method for doing this.

Listing 2-4.

```
private DirContext getContext() throws NamingException{
    Properties environment = new Properties();
    environment.setProperty(DirContext.INITIAL_CONTEXT_FACTORY, "com.sun.jndi.ldap.
    LdapCtxFactory");
    environment.setProperty(DirContext.PROVIDER_URL, "ldap://localhost:10389");
    environment.setProperty(DirContext.SECURITY_PRINCIPAL, "uid=admin,ou=system");
    environment.setProperty(DirContext.SECURITY_CREDENTIALS, "secret");
    DirContext context = new InitialDirContext(environment);
    return context;
}
```

Once we have the initial context, adding the new employee information is a straightforward operation as shown in Listing 2-5.

Listing 2-5.

```java
public void addEmploye(Employee employee) {
   DirContext context = null;
   try {
      context = getContext();
      // Populate the attributes
      Attributes attributes = new BasicAttributes();
      attributes.put(new BasicAttribute("objectClass", "inetOrgPerson"));
      attributes.put(new BasicAttribute("uid", employee.getUid()));
      attributes.put(new BasicAttribute("givenName", employee.getFirstName()));
      attributes.put(new BasicAttribute("surname", employee.getLastName()));
      attributes.put(new BasicAttribute("commonName", employee.getCommonName()));
      attributes.put(new BasicAttribute("departmentNumber",
      employee.getDepartmentNumber()));
      attributes.put(new BasicAttribute("mail", employee.getEmail()));
      attributes.put(new BasicAttribute("employeeNumber",
      employee.getEmployeeNumber()));

      Attribute phoneAttribute = new BasicAttribute("telephoneNumber");
      for(String phone : employee.getPhone()) {
         phoneAttribute.add(phone);
      }
      attributes.put(phoneAttribute);

        // Get the fully  qualified DN
      String dn   =  "uid="+employee.getUid() +  "," +  BASE_PATH;
      // Add  the entry
      context.createSubcontext("dn", attributes);
   }
   catch(NamingException e) {
      // Handle the exception properly
         e.printStackTrace();
   }
   finally {
      closeContext(context);
   }
}
```

As you can see, the first step in the process is to create a set of attributes that needs be added to the entry. JNDI provides the javax.naming.directory.Attributes interface and its implementation javax.naming.directory.BasicAttributes to abstract an attribute collection. We then add the employee's attributes one at a time to the collection using JNDI's javax.naming.directory.BasicAttribute class. Notice that we have taken two approaches in creating the BasicAttribute class. In the first approach we have added the single valued attributes by passing the attribute name and value to BasicAttribute's constructor. To handle the multi-valued attribute telephone, we first created the BasicAttribute instance by just passing in the name. Then we individually added the telephone values to the attribute. Once all the attributes are added, we invoked the createSubcontext method on the initial context to add the entry. The createSubcontext method requires the fully qualified DN of the entry to be added.

Notice that we have delegated the closing of the context to a separate method closeContext. Listing 2-6 shows its implementation.

Listing 2-6.

```
private void closeContext(DirContext context) {
    try {
        if(null != context) {
        context.close();
        }
    }
    catch(NamingException e) {
        // Ignore the  exception
    }
}
```

Updating an Entry

Modifying an existing LDAP entry can involve any of the following operations:

> » Add a new attribute and value(s) or add a new value to an existing multi valued attribute.

> » Replace an existing attribute value(s).

> » Remove an attribute and its value(s).

In order to allow modification of the entries, JNDI provides an aptly named javax. naming.directory.ModificationItem class.

A ModificationItem consists of the type of modification to be made and the attribute under modification. The code below creates a modification item for adding a new telephone number.

```
Attribute telephoneAttribute =  new  BasicAttribute("telephone", "80181001000");
ModificationItem modificationItem  =  new  ModificationItem(DirContext.
ADD_ATTRIBUTE,  telephoneAttribute);
```

Notice that in the above code, we have used the constant ADD_ATTRIBUTE to indicate that we want an add operation. Table 2-2 provides the supported modification types along with their descriptions.

Table 2-2. *LDAP Modification Types*

Modification Type	Description
ADD_ATTRIBUTE	Adds the attribute with the supplied value or values to the entry. If the attribute does not exist then it will be created. If the attribute already exists and the attribute is a multi-valued then this operation simply adds the specified value(s) to the existing list. However, this operation on an existing single valued attributes will result in the AttributeInUseException.
REPLACE_ATTRIBUTE	Replaces existing attribute values of an entry with the supplied values. If the attribute does not exist then it will be created. If the attribute already exists, then all of its values will be replaced.
REMOVE_ATTRIBUTE	Removes the specified value from the existing attribute. If no value is specified then the attribute in its entirety will be removed. If the specified value does not exist in the attribute, the operation will throw a NamingException. If the value to be removed is the only value of the attribute, then the attribute is also removed.

The code for updating an entry is provided in Listing 2-7. The modifyAttributes method takes the fully qualified DN of the entry to be modified and an array of modification items.

Listing 2-7.

```java
public void update(String dn, ModificationItem[] items) {
  DirContext context = null;
  try {
    context = getContext();
    context.modifyAttributes(dn, items);
  }
  catch (NamingException e) {
    e.printStackTrace();
  }
  finally {
    closeContext(context);
  }
}
```

Removing an Entry

Removing an entry using JNDI is again a straightforward process and is shown in Listing 2-8. The destroySubcontext method takes the fully qualified DN of the entry that needs to be deleted.

Listing 2-8.

```
public  void remove(String dn) {
    DirContext context  =  null;
    try  {
        context = getContext();
        context.destroySubcontext(dn);
    }
    catch(NamingException e)  {
        e.printStackTrace();
    finally  {
        closeContext(context);
    }
}
```

Many LDAP servers don't allow an entry to be deleted if it has child entries. In those servers, deleting a non-leaf entry would require traversing the sub tree and deleting all the child entries. Then the non-leaf entry can be deleted. Listing 2-9 shows the code involved in deleting a sub tree.

Listing 2-9.

```
public  void removeSubTree(DirContext ctx, String root)
throws  NamingException {
NamingEnumeration enumeration  =  null;
try  {
    enumeration = ctx.listBindings(root);
    while (enumeration.hasMore())  {
        Binding childEntry =(Binding)enumeration.next();
        LdapName childName  =  new  LdapName(root);
        childName.add(childEntry.getName());

        try  {
            ctx.destroySubcontext(childName);
        }
        catch  (ContextNotEmptyException e)  {
        removeSubTree(ctx, childName.toString());
        ctx.destroySubcontext(childName);
        }
    }
}
catch  (NamingException e)  {
    e.printStackTrace();
}
```

```
finally  {
        try  {
                enumeration.close();
        }
        catch (Exception e)  {
                e.printStackTrace();
        }
    }
}
```

■ **Note**   The OpenDJ LDAP server supports a special sub tree delete control that when attached to a delete request can cause the server to delete the non-leaf entry and all its child entries. We will look at the using LDAP controls in Chapter 7.

Searching Entries

Searching for information is usually the most common operation performed against an LDAP server. In order to perform a search, we need to provide information such as the scope of the search, what we are looking for, and what attributes need to be returned. In JNDI, this search metadata is provided using the SearchControls class. Listing 2-10 provides an example of a search control with subtree scope and returns the givenName and telephoneNumber attributes. The subtree scope indicates that the search should start from the given base entry and should search all its subtree entries. We will look at different scopes available in detail in Chapter 6.

Listing 2-10.

```
SearchControls searchControls  =  new  SearchControls();
searchControls.setSearchScope(SearchControls.SUBTREE_SCOPE);
searchControls.setReturningAttributes(new String[]{"givenName",
"telephoneNumber"});
```

Once we have the search controls defined, the next step is to invoke one of the many search methods in the DirContext instance. Listing 2-11 provides the code that searches all the employees and prints their first name and telephone number.

Listing 2-11.

```
public void search() {
    DirContext context  =  null;
    NamingEnumeration<SearchResult> searchResults = null;
    try
```

```
{
    context =  getContext();
    // Setup Search meta data
    SearchControls searchControls  =  new  SearchControls();
    searchControls.setSearchScope(SearchControls.SUBTREE_SCOPE);
    searchControls.setReturningAttributes(new String[]
    {"givenName",  "telephoneNumber"});
    searchResults =  context.search("dc=inflinx,dc=com",
    "(objectClass=inetOrgPerson)", searchControls);
      while (searchResults.hasMore())  {
        SearchResult result =  searchResults.next();
        Attributes attributes  =  result.getAttributes();
        String firstName =  (String)attributes.get("givenName").get();
        // Read the  multi-valued  attribute
        Attribute  phoneAttribute =  attributes. get("telephoneNumber");
        String[] phone =  new  String[phoneAttribute.size()];
        NamingEnumeration phoneValues  =  phoneAttribute.getAll();
        for(int i =  0;  phoneValues.hasMore(); i++) {
        phone[i] =  (String)phoneValues.next();
        }
    System.out.println(firstName +    ">  " + Arrays.toString(phone));
    }
  }
catch(NamingException e)  {
    e.printStackTrace();
}
finally  {
    try  {
        if (null  != searchResults) {
        searchResults.close();
        }
    closeContext(context);
    } catch  (NamingException e)  {
    // Ignore this
    }
  }
}
```

Here we used the search method with three parameters: a base that determines the starting point of the search, a filter that narrows down the results, and a search control. The search method returns an enumeration of SearchResults. Each search result holds the LDAP entry's attributes. Hence we loop through the search results and read the attribute values. Notice that for multi valued attributes we obtain another enumeration instance and read its values one at a time. In the final part of the code, we close the result enumeration and the context resources.

JNDI Drawbacks

Though JNDI provides a nice abstraction for accessing directory services, it does suffer from several of the following drawbacks:

» Explicit Resource Management

The developer is responsible for closing all the resources. This is very error prone and can result in memory leaks.

» Plumbing Code

The methods we have seen above have lot of plumbing code that can be easily abstracted and reused. This plumbing code makes testing harder and the developer has to learn the nitty-gritty of the API.

» Checked Exceptions

The usage for checked exceptions especially in irrecoverable situations is questionable. Having to explicitly handle NamingException in those scenarios usually results in empty try catch blocks.

CHAPTER 3

■ ■ ■

Introducing Spring LDAP

In this chapter, we will discuss

- The basics of Spring LDAP.

- Downloading and setting up Spring LDAP.

- Setting up the STS development environment.

- Setting up a test LDAP server.

- Creating a Hello World application.

Spring LDAP provides simple, clean and comprehensive support for LDAP programming in Java. This project originally started out on Sourceforge in 2006 under the name LdapTemplate with the intention of simplifying access to LDAP using JNDI. The project later became part of the Spring Framework portfolio and has since come a long way. Figure 3-1 depicts the architecture of a Spring LDAP-based application.

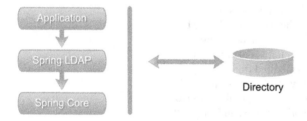

Figure 3-1. *Spring LDAP architecture directory*

The application code uses the Spring LDAP API for performing operations on a LDAP server. The Spring LDAP framework contains all of the LDAP-specific code and abstractions. Spring LDAP, however, will rely on the Spring Framework for some of its infrastructural needs.

The Spring Framework has become today's de facto standard for developing Java-based enterprise applications. Among many other things, it provides a dependency-injection based lightweight alternative to the JEE programming model. The Spring Framework is the base for Spring LDAP and all other Spring portfolio projects such as Spring MVC and Spring Security.

Motivation

In the previous chapter, we discussed the shortcomings of the JNDI API. A notable drawback of JNDI is that it is very verbose; almost all of the code in Chapter 2 has to do with plumbing and very little with application logic. Spring LDAP addresses this problem by providing template and utility classes that take care of the plumbing code so that the developer can focus on business logic.

Another notable issue with JNDI is that it requires the developer to explicitly manage resources such as LDAP contexts. This can be very error-prone. Forgetting to close resources can result in leaks and can quickly bring down an application under heavy load. Spring LDAP manages these resources on your behalf and automatically closes them when you no longer need them. It also provides the ability to pool LDAP contexts, which can improve performance.

Any problems that might arise during the execution of JNDI operations will be reported as instances of NamingException or its subclasses. NamingException is a checked exception and thus the developer is forced to handle it. Data access exceptions are usually not recoverable and most often there is not much that can be done to catch these exceptions. To address this, Spring LDAP provides a consistent unchecked exception hierarchy that mimics NamingException. This allows the application designer to make the choice of when and where to handle these exceptions.

Finally, plain JNDI programming is hard and can be daunting for new developers. Spring LDAP with its abstractions makes working with JNDI more enjoyable. Additionally, it provides a variety of features such as object directory mapping and support for transactions, making it an important tool for any enterprise LDAP developer.

Obtaining Spring LDAP

Before you can install and start using Spring LDAP, it is important to make sure that the Java Development Kit (JDK) is already installed on your machine. The latest Spring LDAP 1.3.2 version requires JDK 1.4 or higher and Spring 2.0 or higher. Since I am using Spring 3.2.4 in the examples in the book, it is strongly recommended to install JDK 6.0 or higher.

Spring Framework and its portfolio projects can be downloaded from www.springsource.org/download/community. A direct link is available on the Spring LDAP web site at www.springsource.org/ldap. The Spring LDAP download page allows you to download the latest as well as previous versions of the framework, as shown in Figure 3-2.

- Spring LDAP
  - Latest GA release: 1.3.2.RELEASE

    spring-ldap-1.3.2.RELEASE-dist.zip (sha1) 3.7 MB

  - More >>

Figure 3-2. *Spring LDAP download*

The spring-ldap-1.3.2.RELEASE-dist.zip includes the framework binaries, source code, and documentation. Since the latest LDAP distribution bundle does not include Spring distributions, you need to separately download Spring Framework. Figure 3-3 shows the latest available Spring Framework distribution, 3.2.4.RELEASE. Download both Spring LDAP and Spring distributions, as shown in Figure 3-3, and unzip them on your machine.

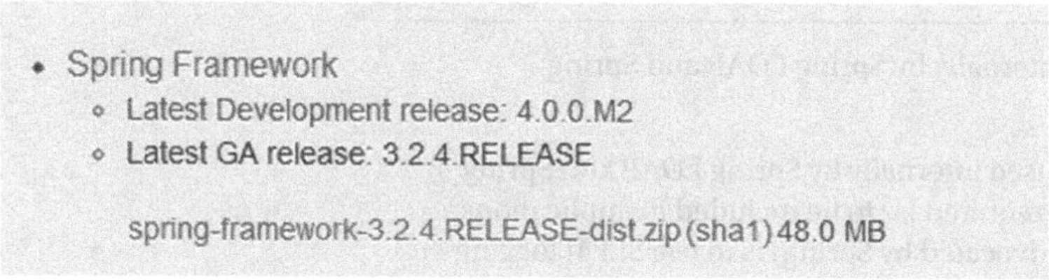

- Spring Framework
    - Latest Development release: 4.0.0.M2
    - Latest GA release: 3.2.4.RELEASE

    spring-framework-3.2.4.RELEASE-dist.zip (sha1) 48.0 MB

Figure 3-3. *Spring Framework download*

Spring LDAP Packaging

Now that you have successfully downloaded the Spring LDAP framework, let's delve into its subfolders. The libs folder contains Spring LDAP binary, source, and javadoc distribution. The LDAP framework is packaged into six different components. Table 3-1 provides a brief description of each component. The docs folder contains the javadoc for the API and the reference guide in different formats.

Table 3-1. *Spring LDAP Distribution Modules*

Component Jar	Description
spring-ldap-core	Contains all the classes necessary for using the LDAP framework. This jar is required in all the applications.
spring-ldap-core-tiger	Contains classes and extensions that are specific to Java 5 and higher. Applications running under Java 5 should not use this jar.
spring-ldap-test	Contains classes and utilities that make testing easier. It also includes classes for starting and stopping in-memory instances of ApacheDS LDAP server.
spring-ldap-ldif-core	Contains classes for parsing ldif format files.
spring-ldap-ldif-batch	Contains classes necessary to integrate ldif parser with Spring Batch Framework.
spring-ldap-odm	Contains classes for enabling and creating object directory mappings.

29

Along with Spring Framework, you need additional jar files for compiling and running applications using Spring LDAP. Table 3-2 lists some of these dependent jars files along with a description of why they are used.

Table 3-2. *Spring LDAP Dependent Jars*

Library Jar	Description
commons-lang	A required jar used internally by Spring LDAP and Spring Framework.
commons-logging	Logging abstraction used internally by Spring LDAP and Spring Framework. This is a required jar to be included in applications. An alternative (and advocated by Spring) is to use SLF4J logging framework using the SLF4J-JCL bridge.
log4j	Required library for logging using Log4J.
spring-core	Spring library that contains core utilities used internally by Spring LDAP. This is a required library for using Spring LDAP.
spring-beans	Spring Framework library used for creating and managing Spring beans. Another library required by Spring LDAP.
spring-context	Spring library that is responsible for dependency injection. This is required when using Spring LDAP inside a Spring application.
spring-tx	Spring Framework library that provides transaction abstractions. This is required when using Spring LDAP transaction support.
spring-jdbc	Library that simplifies access to database using JDBC under the covers. This is an optional library and should be used for transaction support.
commons-pool	Apache Commons Pool library provides support for pooling. This should be included when using Spring LDAP pooling support.
ldapbp	Sun LDAP booster pack that includes additional LDAP V3 Server controls. This jar is needed when you are planning to use these additional controls or running under Java 5 or lower.

Downloading Spring LDAP Source

The Spring LDAP project uses Git as their source control system. The source code can be downloaded from https://github.com/SpringSource/spring-ldap.

Spring LDAP source code can provide valuable insights into the framework architecture. It also includes a rich test suite that can serve as additional documentation and help you understand the framework. I strongly recommend that you download and look at the source code. The Git repository also holds a sandbox folder that contains several experimental features that may or may not make it into the framework.

Installing Spring LDAP Using Maven

Apache Maven is an open source, standards-based project management framework that makes building, testing, reporting, and packaging of projects easier. If you are new to Maven and are wondering about the tool, the Maven web site, http://maven.apache.org, provides information on its features along with tons of helpful links. Here are some advantages of adopting Maven:

- *Standardized directory structure*: Maven standardizes the layout and organization of a project. Every time a new project starts, considerable time is spent on decisions such as where the source code should go or where the configuration files should be placed. Also, these decisions can vary vastly between projects and teams. Maven's standardized directory structure makes adoption easy across developers and even IDEs.

- *Declarative dependency management*: With Maven, you declare your project dependencies in a separate pom.xml file. Maven then automatically downloads those dependencies from repositories and uses them during build process. Maven also smartly resolves and downloads transitive dependencies (dependencies of dependencies).

- *Archetypes*: Maven archetypes are project templates that can be used to easily generate new projects. These archetypes are great way to share best practices and enforce consistency beyond Maven's standard directory structure.

- *Plug-ins*: Maven follows a plug-in based architecture that makes it easy to add or customize its functionality. Currently there are hundreds of plug-ins that can be used to carry out variety of tasks from compiling code to creating project documentation. Activating and using a plug-in simply involves declaring a reference to the plug-in in the pom.xml file.

- *Tools support*: All major IDEs today provide tooling support for Maven. This includes wizards for generating projects, creating IDE-specific files, and graphical tools for analyzing dependencies.

Installing Maven

To install Maven, simply download the latest version from http://maven.apache.org/download.html. Once the download is complete, unzip the distribution to a local directory on your machine. Then make the following modifications to your development box:

- Add a M2_HOME environment variable pointing to the maven installation directory.

- Add a MAVEN_OPTS environment variable with the value of – Xmx512m.

- Add to the Path environment variable the M2_HOME/bin value.

■ **Note** Maven requires an Internet connection for downloading dependencies and plug-ins. If you or your company uses a proxy to connect to Internet, make changes to the `settings.xml` file. Otherwise you may experience "Unable to download artifact" errors.

This completes Maven installation. You can verify the installation by running the following command on your command line:

```
$ mvn -v
```

This command should output information similar to the following:

```
Apache Maven 3.1.0 (893ca28a1da9d5f51ac03827af98bb730128f9f2; 2013-06-27
20:15:32-0600)
Maven home: c:\tools\maven
Java version: 1.6.0_35, vendor: Sun Microsystems Inc.
Java home: C:\Java\jdk1.6.0_35\jre
Default locale: en_US, platform encoding: Cp1252
OS name: "windows 7", version: "6.1", arch: "x86", family: "windows"
```

Spring LDAP Archetypes

To jump-start Spring LDAP development, this book uses the following two archetypes:

- practical-ldap-empty-archetype: This archetype can be used to create an empty Java project with all the required LDAP dependencies.

- practical-ldap-archetype: Similar to the above archetype, this archetype creates a Java project with all the required LDAP dependencies. Additionally, it also includes Spring LDAP configuration files, sample code, and dependencies to run an in-memory LDAP server for testing purposes.

Before you can use the archetypes to create a project, you need to install them. If you have not already done so, download the accompanying source/download files from Apress. In the downloaded distribution, you will find `practical-ldap-empty-archetype-1.0.0.jar` and `practical-ldap-archetype-1.0.0.jar` archetypes. Once you have the jar files downloaded, run the following two commands at the command line:

```
mvn install:install-file \
    -DgroupId=com.inflinx.book.ldap \
    -DartifactId=practical-ldap-empty-archetype \
    -Dversion=1.0.0 \
    -Dpackaging=jar \
    -Dfile=<JAR_LOCATION_DOWNLOAD>/practical-ldap-empty-archetype-1.0.0.jar
```

```
mvn   install:install-file \
      -DgroupId=com.inflinx.book.ldap \
      -DartifactId=practical-ldap-archetype \
      -Dversion=1.0.0 \
      -Dpackaging=jar
      -Dfile=< JAR_LOCATION_DOWNLOAD >/practical-ldap-archetype-1.0.0.jar
```

These maven install commands will install the two archetypes in your local maven repository. Creating a project using one of these archetypes simply involves running the following command:

```
C:\practicalldap\code>mvn archetype:generate
-DarchetypeGroupId=com.inflinx.book.ldap \
-DarchetypeArtifactId=practical-ldap-empty-archetype \
-DarchetypeVersion=1.0.0 \
-DgroupId=com.inflinx.ldap \
-DartifactId=chapter3 \
-DinteractiveMode=false
```

Notice that this command is executed inside the directory c:/practicalldap/code. The command instructs maven to use the archetype practical-ldap-empty-archetype and generate a project named chapter3. The generated project directory structure is shown in Figure 3-4.

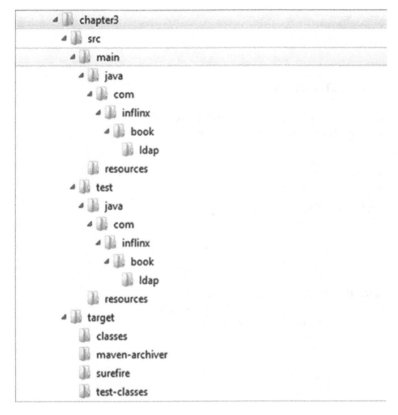

Figure 3-4. *Maven-generated project structure*

This directory structure has a src folder that holds all the code and any associated resources such as XML files. The target folder contains the generated classes and build artifacts. The main folder under src usually holds the code that eventually makes its way to production. The test folder contains the related test code. Each of these two folders contains java and resources subfolders. As name suggests, the java folder contains Java code and the resources folder usually contains configuration xml files.

The pom.xml file in the root folder holds the configuration information needed by Maven. For example, it contains information about all the dependent jar files that are required for compiling the code (see Listing 3-1).

Listing 3-1.

```
<dependencies>
    <dependency>
        <groupId>org.springframework.ldap</groupId>
        <artifactId>spring-ldap-core</artifactId>
```

```
        <version>${org.springframework.ldap.version}</version>
        <scope>compile</scope>
    </dependency>
</dependencies>
```

The pom.xml snippet in Listing 3-1 indicates that the project will need the spring-ldap-core.jar file during its compilation.

Maven requires a group id and artifact id to uniquely identify a dependency. A group id is usually unique to a project or organization and is similar to the concept of a Java package. The artifact id is usually the name of the project or a generated component of the project. The scope determines the phase during which the dependency should be included in the classpath. Here are few possible values:

- *test*: A test scope indicates that the dependency should be included in the classpath only during testing process. JUnit is an example of such dependency.

- *provided*: The provided scope indicates that the artifact should be included in the classpath during compilation only. Provided scope dependencies are usually available at runtime via JDK or application container.

- *compile*: A compile scope indicates that the dependency should be included in the classpath at all times.

An additional section in the pom.xml file contains information about the plug-ins that Maven can use to compile and build the code. One such plug-in declaration is displayed in Listing 3-2. It instructs Maven to use the compiler plug-in of version 2.0.2 to compile Java code. The finalName indicates the name of the generated artifact. In this case, it would be chapter3.jar.

Listing 3-2.

```
<build>
    <plugins>
        <plugin>
            <groupId>org.apache.maven.plugins</groupId>
            <artifactId>maven-compiler-plugin
            </artifactId>
            <version>2.0.2</version>
            <configuration>
                <source>1.6</source>
                <target>1.6</target>
            </configuration>
        </plugin>
    </plugins>
    <finalName>chapter3</finalName>
</build>
```

To build this generated application, simply run the following command from the command line. This command cleans the target folder, compiles the source files, and generates a jar file inside the target folder.

```
mvn  clean  compile package
```

This setup, along with a text editor, is enough to start developing and packaging Java-based LDAP applications. However, it is a no-brainer that you can be more productive developing and debugging applications using a graphical IDE. There are several IDEs, with Eclipse, NetBeans, and IntelliJ IDEA being the most popular. For this book you will be using Spring Tool Suite, an Eclipse-based IDE from Spring Source.

Setting Up Spring IDE

STS is a free, Eclipse-based development environment that provides the best tool support for developing Spring-based applications. The following are some of its features:

- Wizards for creating Spring projects and Spring beans

- Integrated support for Maven

- Templates based on best practices for project and file creation

- Spring bean and AOP pointcut visualization

- Spring ROO shell integration for rapid prototyping

- Task-based user interface that provides guided assistance through tutorials

- Support for Groovy and Grails

In this section you will look at installing and setting up the STS IDE.

1. Download and initiate the STS installer from the Spring Tool Suite web site at www.springsource.com/developer/sts. The installation file for Windows is spring-tool-suite-3.3.0.RELEASE-e4.3-win32-installer.exe. Double-click the install file to start the installation (Figure 3-5).

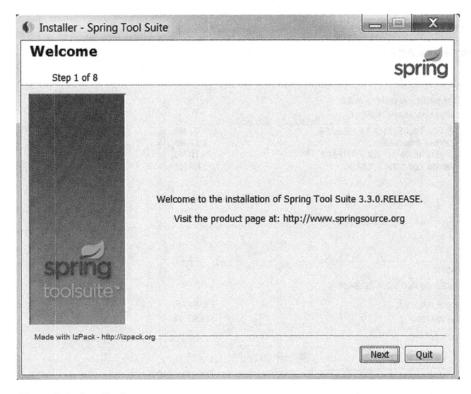

Figure 3-5. *Installer home screen*

2. Read and accept the License Agreement and click the Next button.

3. On the Target Path screen, choose an installation directory.

4. Leave the default selection and then click the Next button (see Figure 3-6).

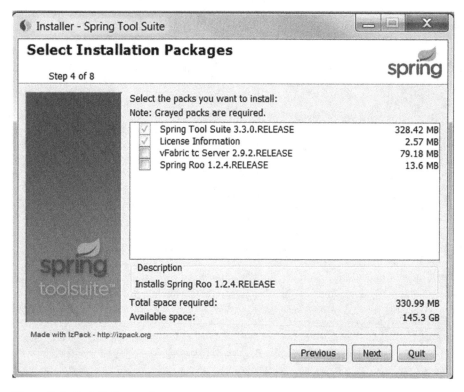

Figure 3-6. *Installation packages*

5. On the following screen, provide the path to the JDK installation and click the Next button.

6. This will begin the installation; wait for the file transfer to complete.

7. Click the Next button on the following two screens to complete the installation.

Creating Projects Using STS

In the earlier "Spring LDAP Archetype" section you used the practical-ldap-empty-archetype archetype to generate a project from command line. Now let's look at generating the same project using STS.

1. From the File menu, select New ➤ Project. It will launch the New Project wizard (see Figure 3-7). Select the Maven Project option and click the Next button.

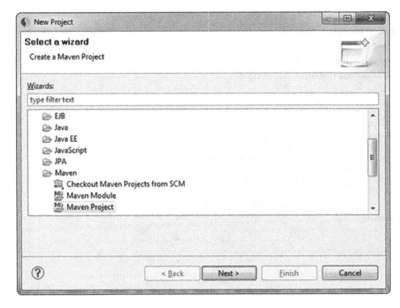

Figure 3-7. *New Project wizard*

2. Uncheck "Use default Workspace location" and enter the path for the newly generated project, and then select the Next button (see Figure 3-8).

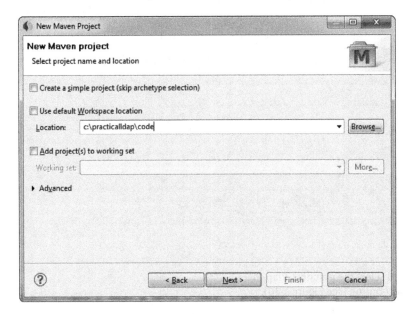

Figure 3-8. *Project path setup*

3. On the Select an Archetype screen (see Figure 3-9), click "Add Archetype." This step assumes that you have already installed the archetype as mentioned in the earlier section. Fill the Add Archetype dialog with the details shown in Figure 3-9 and press OK. Do the same for the other archetype.

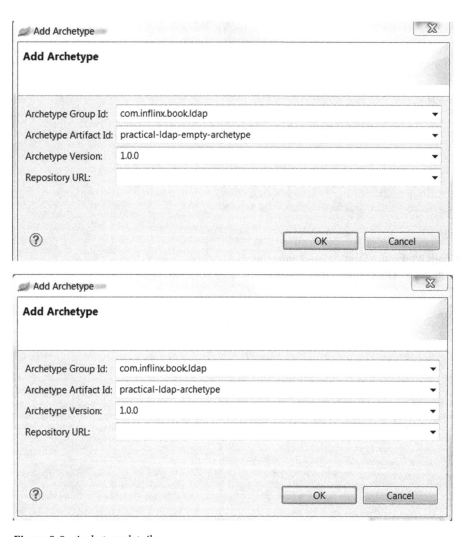

Figure 3-9. *Archetype details*

4. Enter ldap in the Filter field and select the practical-ldap-empty-archetype. Click the Next button (see Figure 3-10).

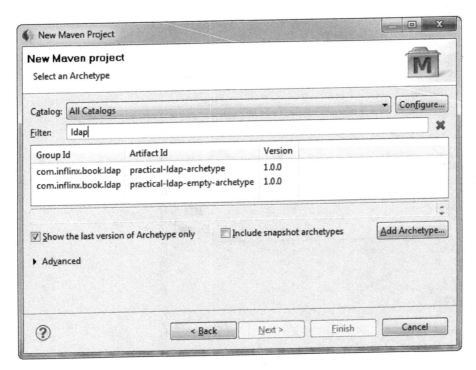

Figure 3-10. *Archetype selection*

5. On the following screen, provide the information about the newly created project and click the Finish button (see Figure 3-11).

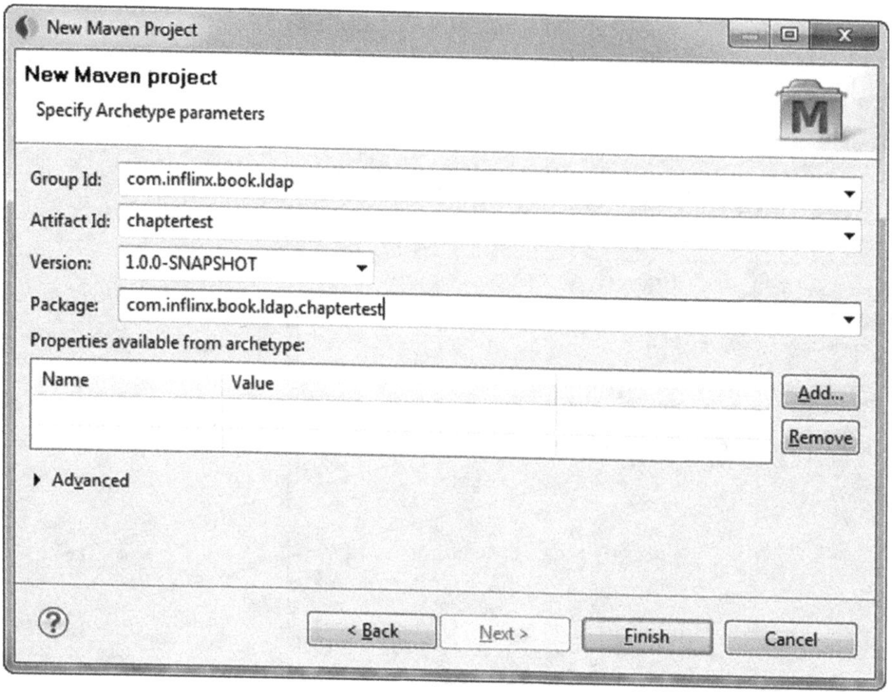

Figure 3-11. Project information

This will generate a project with the same directory structure that you saw earlier. However, it also creates all the IDE-specific files such as .project and .classpath and adds all the dependent Jars to the project's classpath. The complete project structure is shown in Figure 3-12.

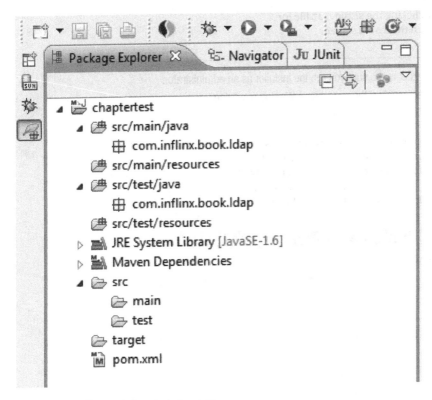

Figure 3-12. *Generated project structure*

LDAP Server Setup

In this section you will look at installing an LDAP server to test your LDAP code. Among the available open source LDAP servers, I find OpenDJ very easy to install and configure.

■ **Note**   Even if you already have a test LDAP server available, I highly recommend that you follow the steps below and install OpenDJ LDAP server. You will be heavily using this instance to test the code in this book.

Download the OpenDJ distribution file OpenDJ-2.4.6.zip from www.forgerock.org/opendj-archive.html. Unzip the distribution to a folder on your local system. On my Windows box, I placed the extracted files and folders under C:\practicalldap\opendj. Then follow these steps to complete the installation.

1. Start the installation by clicking the setup.bat file for Windows. This will launch the install screen.

■ **Note**   When installing under Windows 8, make sure you run the installer as an administrator. Otherwise, you will run into an error when enabling the server as a Windows service.

---

2. On the Server settings screen, enter the following values and press the Next button. I changed the Listener Port from 389 to 11389 and Administration Connector Port from 4444 to 4445. I also used opendj as the password. Please use these settings for running code examples used in this book (see Figure 3-13).

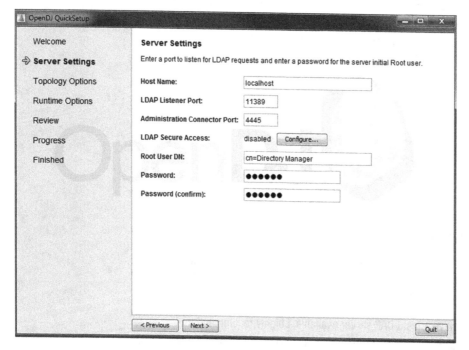

Figure 3-13. *LDAP server settings*

3. In the Topology Option screen, leave the "This will be a standalone server" option and click the Next button.

4. In the Directory Data screen, enter the value "dc=inflinx,dc=com" as the Directory Base DN, leave the other options untouched, and continue.

5. In the Review screen, confirm that "Run the server as a Windows Service" option is checked and click the Finish button.

6. You will see a confirmation indicating a successful installation (see Figure 3-14).

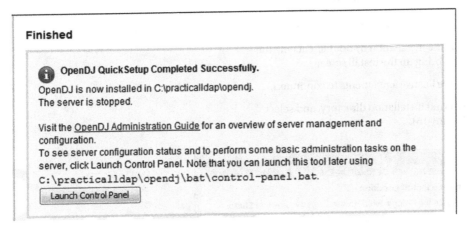

Figure 3-14. *Successful OpenDJ confirmation*

Since you have the OpenDJ installed as Windows Service, you can start the LDAP server by going to Control Panel ➤ Administrative Tools ➤ Services and selecting OpenDJ and clicking Start (Figure 3-15).

Name	Description	Status	Startup Type	Log On As
Offline Files	The Offline ...	Started	Automatic	Local Syste...
OpenDJ	Next Genera...		Automatic	Local Syste...
...	Thi........		M......	L...l C......

Figure 3-15. *Running OpenDJ as a Windows Service*

■ **Note** If you have not installed the OpenDJ as a Windows Service you can start and stop the server using `start-ds.bat` and `stop-ds.bat` files under `<OpenDJ_Install_Folder>/bat` folder.

Installing Apache Directory Studio

The Apache Directory Studio is a popular, open source LDAP browser that can help you browse LDAP directories very easily. To install Apache Directory Studio, download the installer file from

`http://directory.apache.org/studio/downloads.html.`

The Studio installation can be done by following these steps.

1. On Windows, start the installation by double-clicking the install file (this will bring up the install screen).

2. Read and accept the license agreements to continue.

3. Choose your preferred installation directory, and select "Install" (see Figure 3-16).

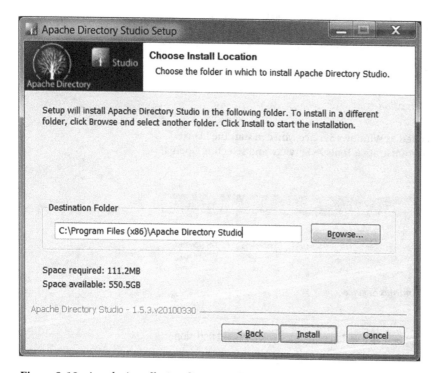

Figure 3-16. *Apache installation directory selection*

4. You will be shown the status of the installation and file transfer.

5. After all the files have been transferred, click the Finish button to complete the installation.

Once the installation is complete, the next step is to create a connection to the newly installed OpenDJ LDAP server. Before you can proceed, make sure your OpenDJ server is running. Here are the steps to set up the new connection.

1. Launch ApacheDS server. In Windows, click the Apache Directory Studio.exe file.

2. Launch the New Connection wizard by right-clicking in the "Connections" section and selecting "New Connection."

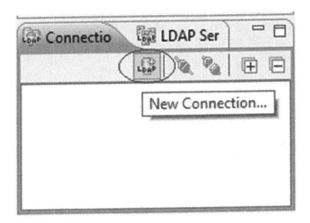

Figure 3-17. *Creating a new connection*

3. On the Network Parameter screen, enter the information displayed in Figure 3-18. This should match the OpenDJ information you entered during OpenDJ installation.

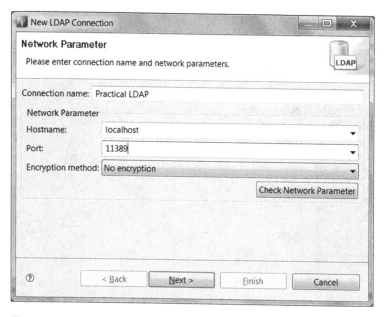

Figure 3-18. *LDAP connection network parameters*

4. On the Authentication screen, enter "cn=Directory Manager" as Bind DN or user and "opendj" as password (see Figure 3-19).

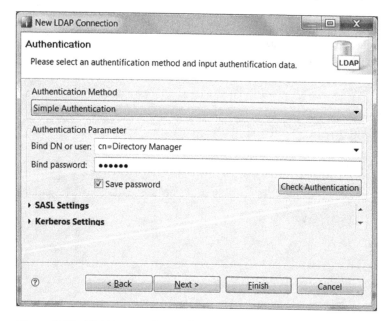

Figure 3-19. *LDAP connection authentication*

5. Accept the defaults in the Browser Options section and select the Finish button.

Loading Test Data

In the previous sections you installed the OpenDJ LDAP server and Apache Directory Studio for accessing the LDAP server. The final step in setting up your development/test environment is to load the LDAP server with test data.

■ **Note**   The accompanying source code/downloads contains two LDIF files, `patrons.ldif` and `employees.ldif`. The `patrons.ldif` file contains test data that mimics your library's patrons. The `employees.ldif` file contains test data that mimics your library's employees. These two files are heavily used for testing the code used in this book. If you have not already done, please download these files before moving forward.

Here are the steps for loading the test data.

1. Right-click "Root DSE" in the LDAP browser pane and select Import ➤ LDIF Import (see Figure 3-20).

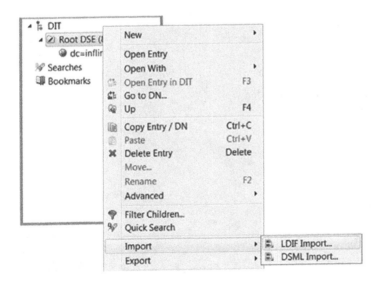

Figure 3-20. LDIF import

2. Browse for this patrons.ldif file (see Figure 3-21) and click the Finish button. Make sure that the "Update existing entries" checkbox is selected.

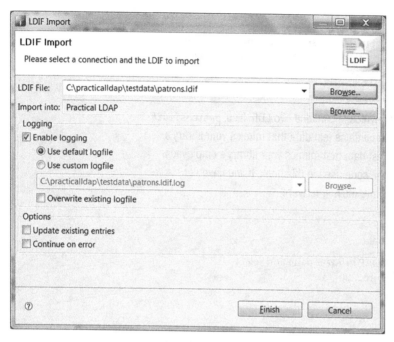

Figure 3-21. *LDIF import settings*

3. Upon a successful import you will see the data loaded under the dc=inflinx,dc=com entry (see Figure 3-22).

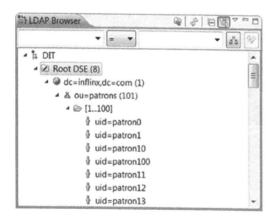

Figure 3-22. *LDIF successful import*

Spring LDAP Hello World

With this information in hand let's dive into the world of Spring LDAP. You will start by writing a simple search client that reads all the patron names in the ou=patrons LDAP branch. This is similar to the example you looked at in Chapter 2. Listing 3-3 shows the search client code.

Listing 3-3.

```
public class SearchClient {

    @SuppressWarnings("unchecked")
    public List<String> search() {
        LdapTemplate ldapTemplate = getLdapTemplate();
        List<String> nameList = ldapTemplate.search( "dc=inflinx,dc=com",
        "(objectclass=person)",
                    new AttributesMapper() {
                        @Override
                        public Object mapFromAttributes(Attributes attributes)
                        throws NamingException {
                            return (String)attributes.get("cn").get();
                        }
                    });
        return nameList;
    }

    private LdapTemplate getLdapTemplate() { ....... }
}
```

Central to Spring LDAP framework is the org.springframework.ldap.core.LdapTemplate class. Based on the Template Method design pattern (http://en.wikipedia.org/wiki/Template_method_pattern), the LdapTemplate class takes care of the unnecessary plumbing involved in LDAP programming. It provides a number of overloaded search, lookup, bind, authenticate, and unbind methods that makes LDAP development a breeze. The LdapTemplate is threadsafe and the same instance can be used by concurrent threads.

SIMPLELDAPTEMPLATE

Spring LDAP version 1.3 introduced a variation of LdapTemplate called SimpleLdapTemplate. This is a Java 5-based convenience wrapper for the classic LdapTemplate. The SimpleLdapTemplate adds Java 5 Generics support to lookup and search methods. These methods now take implementations of ParameterizedContextMapper<T> as parameter, allowing the search and lookup methods to return typed objects.

The SimpleLdapTemplate exposes only a subset of operations available in LdapTemplate. These operations, however, are the most commonly used ones and hence SpringLdapTemplate would be sufficient in a lot of situations. The SimpleLdapTemplate also provides the getLdapOperations() method that exposes the wrapped LdapOperations instance and can be used to invoke the less commonly used template methods.

In this book, you'll use both LdapTemplate and SimpleLdapTemplate classes for implementing code.

You start the search method implementation by obtaining an instance of LdapTemplate class. Then you invoke a variation of the LdapTemplate's search method. The first parameter to the search method is the LDAP base and the second parameter is the search filter. The search method uses the base and filter to perform search and each javax.naming.directory.SearchResult obtained is supplied to an implementation of org.springframework.ldap.core.AttributesMapper that is provided as the third parameter. In Listing 3-3, the AttributesMapper implementation is achieved via creating an anonymous class that reads each SearchResult entry and returns the common name of the entry.

In Listing 3-3, the getLdapTemplate method is empty. Now let's look at implementing this method. For LdapTemplate to properly execute the search it needs an initial context on the LDAP server. Spring LDAP provides org.springframework.ldap.core.ContextSource interface abstraction and its implementation org.springframework.ldap.core.support. LdapContextSource for configuring and creating context instances. Listing 3-4 shows the complete method for getLdapTemplate implementation.

Listing 3-4.

```
private LdapTemplate getLdapTemplate() {
    LdapContextSource contextSource = new LdapContextSource();
    contextSource.setUrl("ldap://localhost:11389");
    contextSource.setUserDn("cn=Directory Manager");
    contextSource.setPassword("opendj");
    try {
        contextSource.afterPropertiesSet();
    }
    catch(Exception e) {
        e.printStackTrace();
    }
    LdapTemplate ldapTemplate = new LdapTemplate();
    ldapTemplate.setContextSource(contextSource);
    return ldapTemplate;
}
```

You start the method implementation by creating a new `LdapContextSource` and populating it with information about the LDAP server, such as the server URL and binding credentials. You then invoke the `afterPropertiesSet` method on the Context Source that allows Spring LDAP perform housekeeping operations. Finally, you create a new `LdapTemplate` instance and pass in the newly created context source.

This completes your search client example. Listing 3-5 shows the main method that invokes the search operation and prints the names to the console.

Listing 3-5.

```
public static void main(String[] args) {
   SearchClient client = new SearchClient();
   List<String> names = client.search();
   for(String name: names) {
      System.out.println(name);
   }
}
```

This search client implementation simply uses Spring LDAP API without any Spring Framework-specific paradigms. In the coming sections, you will look at springifying this application. But before you do that, let's quickly look at Spring ApplicationContext.

Spring ApplicationContext

Central to every Spring Framework application is the notion of ApplicationContext. Implementations of this interface are responsible for creating and configuring Spring beans. The application context also acts as an IoC container and is responsible for performing the dependency injection. A Spring bean is simply a standard POJO with metadata needed to run inside the Spring container.

In a standard Spring application the ApplicationContext is configured via an XML file or Java annotations. Listing 3-6 shows a sample application context file with one bean declaration. The bean `myBean` is of type `com.inflinx.book.ldap.SimplePojo`. When the application loads the context, Spring creates an instance of `SimplePojo` and manages it.

Listing 3-6.

```
<?xml version="1.0"  encoding="UTF-8"?>
<beans xmlns="http://www.springframework.org/schema/beans"
       xmlns:xsi="http://www.w3.org/2001/XMLSchema-instance"
       xmlns:context="http://www.springframework.org/schema/context"
       xsi:schemaLocation="http://www.springframework.org/schema/
beans http://www.springframework.org/schema/beans/spring-beans.xsd
       http://www.springframework.org/schema/context
http://www. springframework.org/schema/context/spring-context.xsd">
```

```
        <bean  id="myBean" class="com.inflinx.book.ldap.SimplePojo">
        </bean>
</beans>
```

Spring-Powered Search Client

Our conversion of the search client implementation begins with the applicationContext.xml file as shown in Listing 3-7.

Listing 3-7.

```
<beans xmlns="http://www.springframework.org/schema/beans"
xmlns:xsi="http://www.w3.org/2001/XMLSchema-instance"
xmlns:context="http://www.springframework.org/schema/context"
xsi:schemaLocation="http://www.springframework.org/schema/beans
http://www.springframework.org/schema/beans/spring-beans.xsd
http://www.springframework.org/schema/context
http://www.springframework.org/schema/context
/spring-context.xsd">

<bean id="contextSource"
class="org.springframework.ldap.core.support.LdapContextSource">
    <property  name="url" value="ldap://localhost:11389"  />
    <property name="userDn" value="cn=Directory  Manager" />
    <property name="password" value="opendj"  />
  </bean>

<bean id="ldapTemplate"
class="org.springframework.ldap.core.LdapTemplate">
    <constructor-arg ref="contextSource" />
</bean>
<context:component-scan base-package="com.inflinx.book.ldap"/>
</beans>
```

In the context file, you declare a contextSource bean to manage connections to LDAP server. For LdapContextSource to properly create instances of DirContext, you need to provide it with information about the LDAP server. The url property takes the fully qualified URL (ldap://server:port format) to the LDAP server. The base property can be used to specify the root suffix for all LDAP operations. The userDn and password properties are used to provide authentication information. Next, you configure a new LdapTemplate bean and inject the contextSource bean.

With all your dependencies declared in the context file, you can proceed to re-implementing the search client, as shown in Listing 3-8.

Listing 3-8.

```java
package com.inflinx.book.ldap;
import java.util.List;
import javax.naming.NamingException;
import javax.naming.directory.Attributes;
import org.springframework.beans.factory.annotation.Autowired;
import org.springframework.beans.factory.annotation.Qualifier;
import org.springframework.context.ApplicationContext;
import org.springframework.context.support. ClassPathXmlApplicationContext;
import org.springframework.ldap.core.AttributesMapper;
import org.springframework.ldap.core.LdapTemplate;
import org.springframework.stereotype.Component;

@Component
public class SpringSearchClient {

    @Autowired
    @Qualifier("ldapTemplate")
    private LdapTemplate ldapTemplate;

    @SuppressWarnings("unchecked")
    public List<String> search() {
        List<String> nameList = ldapTemplate.search("dc=inflinx,dc=com",
        "(objectclass=person)",
                    new AttributesMapper() {
                      @Override
                      public Object mapFromAttributes(Attributes attributes)
                      throws NamingException {
                          return (String)attributes.get("cn").get();
                      }
                  });
        return nameList;
    }
}
```

You will notice that this code is no different from the SearchClient code you saw in Listing 3-4. You just extracted the creation of LdapTemplate to an external configuration file. The @Autowired annotation instructs Spring to inject the ldapTemplate dependency. This simplifies the search client class very much and helps you focus on the search logic.

The code to run the new search client is shown in Listing 3-9. You start by creating a new instance of ClassPathXmlApplicationContext. The ClassPathXmlApplicationContext takes the applicationContext.xml file as its parameter. Then you retrieve an instance of SpringSearchClient from the context and invoke the search method.

Listing 3-9.

```
public static void main(String[] args){
    ApplicationContext context = new ClassPathXmlApplicationContext
    ("classpath:applicationContext.xml");
    SpringSearchClient client = context.getBean(SpringSearchClient.class);
    List<String> names = client.search();
    for(String name: names) {
        System.out.println(name);
    }
}
```

Spring LdapTemplate Operations

In the previous section, you utilized LdapTemplate to implement search. Now, let's look at using LdapTemplate for adding, removing, and modifying information in LDAP.

Add Operation

The LdapTemplate class provides several bind methods that allow you to create new LDAP entries. The simplest among those methods is as follows:

```
public void bind(String dn, Object obj,  Attributes  attributes)
```

The first parameter to this method is the unique distinguished name of the object that needs to be bound. The second parameter is the object to be bound and is usually an implementation of the DirContext interface. The third parameter is the attribute of the object to be bound. Among the three, only the first parameter is required and you can pass a null for the rest of the two.

Listing 3-10 shows the code involved in creating a new patron entry with minimal set of information. You start the method implementation by creating a new instance of BasicAttributes class to hold the patron attributes. Single-valued attributes are added by passing the attribute name and value to the put method. To add the multi-valued attribute objectclass, you create a new instance of BasicAttribute. You then add the entry's objectClass values to the objectClassAttribute and add it to the attributes list. Finally, you invoke the bind method on the LdapTemplate with the patron information and patron's fully qualified DN. This adds the patron entry to LDAP server.

Listing 3-10.

```
public void addPatron() {
    // Set the Patron attributes
    Attributes attributes = new BasicAttributes();
    attributes.put("sn", "Patron999");
    attributes.put("cn", "New Patron999");
```

```
// Add the multi-valued attribute
BasicAttribute objectClassAttribute = new BasicAttribute("objectclass");
objectClassAttribute.add("top");
objectClassAttribute.add("person");
objectClassAttribute.add("organizationalperson");
objectClassAttribute.add("inetorgperson");
attributes.put(objectClassAttribute);
ldapTemplate.bind("uid=patron999,ou=patrons,dc=inflinx,dc=com",null,
attributes);
}
```

Modify Operation

Consider the scenario where you want to add a telephone number to the newly added patron. To do that, LdapTemplate provides a convenient modifyAttributes method with the following signature:

```
public void modifyAttributes(String dn, ModificationItem[]  mods)
```

This variation of modifyAttributes method takes the fully qualified unique DN of the entry to be modified as its first parameter. The second parameter takes an array of ModificationItems where each modification item holds the attribute information that needs to be modified.

Listing 3-11 shows the code that adds a new telephone number to the patron.

Listing 3-11.

```
public void addTelephoneNumber() {
    Attribute attribute = new BasicAttribute("telephoneNumber", "801 100 1000");
    ModificationItem item = new ModificationItem(DirContext.ADD_ATTRIBUTE,
    attribute);
    ldapTemplate.modifyAttributes("uid=patron999," +
    "ou=patrons,dc=inflinx,dc=com", new ModificationItem[] {item});
}
```

In this implementation, you simply create a new BasicAttribute with telephone information. Then you create a new ModificationItem and pass in the ADD_ATTRIBUTE code, indicating that you are adding an attribute. Finally, you invoke the modifyAttributes method with the patron DN and the modification item. The DirContext has a REPLACE_ATTRIBUTE code that when used will replace an attribute's value. Similarly, the REMOVE_ATTRIBUTE code will remove the specified value from the attribute.

Deleting Operation

Similar to addition and modification, LdapTemplate makes it easy to remove an entry with the unbind method. Listing 3-12 provides the code that implements the unbind method and removes a patron. As you can see, the unbind method takes the DN for the entry that needs to be removed.

Listing 3-12.

```
public void removePatron() {
    ldapTemplate.unbind("uid=patron999," + "ou=patrons,dc=inflinx,dc=com");
}
```

Summary

Spring LDAP Framework aims at simplifying LDAP programming in Java. In this chapter, you got a high-level overview of Spring LDAP and some of the concepts associated with Spring Framework. You also looked at the setup needed to get up and running with Spring LDAP. In the next chapter, you will focus on testing Spring LDAP applications.

CHAPTER 4

Testing LDAP Code

In this chapter, you will learn

- The basics of unit/mock/integration testing.
- Testing using an embedded LDAP server.
- Mock testing using EasyMock.
- Generating test data.

Testing is an important aspect of any software development process. As well as detecting bugs, it also helps to verify that all requirements are met and that the software works as expected. Today, formally or informally, testing is included in almost every phase of the software development process. Depending on what is being tested and the purpose behind the test, we end up with several different types of testing. The most common testing done by developers is unit testing, which ensures that individual units are working as expected. Integration testing usually follows unit testing and focuses on the interaction between previously tested components. Developers are usually involved in creating automated integration tests, especially the tests that deal with databases and directories. Next is system testing where the complete, integrated system is evaluated to ensure that all the requirements have been met. Non-functional requirements such as performance and efficiency are also tested as part of system testing. Acceptance testing is usually done at the end to make sure that the delivered software meets the customer/business user needs.

Unit Testing

Unit testing is a testing methodology where the smallest parts of the application, referred to as units, are verified and validated individually in isolation. In structural programming, the unit could be an individual method or function. In object-oriented programming (OOP), an object is the smallest executable unit. Interaction between objects is central to any OO design and is usually done by invoking methods. Thus, unit testing in OOP can range from testing individual methods to testing a cluster of objects.

Writing unit tests requires a developer's time and effort. But this investment has been proven to deliver several undeniable benefits.

■ **Note** It is important to measure how much of the code is covered by unit tests. Tools like Clover and Emma provide metrics for code coverage. These metrics can also be used to highlight any paths that are exercised by few unit tests (or none at all).

The biggest advantage of unit testing is that it can help identify bugs at early stages of development. Bugs that are discovered only during QA or in production consume a lot more debugging time and money. Also, a good set of unit tests acts as a safety net and gives confidence when code is refactored. Unit tests can help improve design and even serve as documentation.

Good unit tests have the following characteristics:

- Every unit test must be independent of other tests. This atomic nature is very important and each test must not cause any side effects to other tests. Unit tests should also be order independent.

- A unit test must be repeatable. For a unit test to be of any value, it must produce consistent results. Otherwise, it cannot be used as a sanity check during refactoring.

- Unit tests must be easy to set up and clean up. So they should not rely on external systems such as databases and servers.

- Unit tests must be fast and provide immediate feedback. It would not be productive to wait on long-running tests before you make another change.

- Unit tests must be self-validating. Each test should contain enough information to determine automatically if a test passes or fails. No manual intervention should be needed to interpret the results.

Enterprise applications often use external systems like databases, directories, and web services. This is especially true in the DAO layer. Unit testing database code, for example, may involve starting a database server, loading it with schema and data, running tests, and shutting down the server. This quickly becomes tricky and complex. One approach is to use mock objects and hide the external dependencies. Where this is not sufficient, it may be necessary to use integration testing and test the code with external dependencies intact. Let's look at each case in little more detail.

Mock Testing

The goal of mock testing is to use mock objects to simulate real objects in controlled ways. Mock objects implement the same interface as that of the real objects but are scripted to mimic/fake and track their behavior.

For example, consider a UserAccountService that has a method to create new user accounts. The implementation of such a service usually involves validating the account information against business rules, storing the newly created account in a database, and sending out a confirmation e-mail. Persisting data and e-mailing information are usually abstracted out to classes in other layers. Now, when writing a unit test to validate the business rules associated with the account creation, you might not really care about the intricacies involved in the e-mail notification part. However, you do want to verify that an e-mail got generated. This is exactly where mock objects come in handy. To achieve this, you just need to give the UserAccountService a mock implementation of the EmailService that is responsible for sending e-mails. The mock implementation will simply mark the e-mail request and return a hardcoded result. Mock objects are a great way to isolate tests from complex dependencies, allowing them to run faster.

There are several open source frameworks that make working with mock objects easier. Popular ones include Mockito, EasyMock, and JMock. A complete comparison list of these frameworks can be found at http://code.google.com/p/jmockit/wiki/MockingToolkitComparisonMatrix.

Some of these frameworks allow creating mocks for classes that don't implement any interfaces. Regardless of the framework used, unit testing using mock objects usually involves the following steps:

- Create a new mock instance.

- Set up the mock. This involves instructing the mock what to expect and what to return.

- Run the tests, passing the mock instance to the component under test.

- Verify the results.

Integration Testing

Even though mock objects serve as great placeholders, very soon you will run into cases where faking will not be enough. This is especially true for DAO layer code where you need to validate SQL query executions and verify modifications to database records. Testing this kind of code falls under the umbrella of integration testing. As mentioned earlier, integration testing focuses on testing interactions between components with their dependencies in place.

It has become common for developers to write automated integration tests using unit-testing tools, thereby blurring the distinction between the two. However, it is important to remember that integration tests don't run in isolation and are usually slower. Frameworks such as Spring provide container support for writing and executing integration tests easily. The improved availability of embedded databases, directories, and servers enables developers to write faster integration tests.

JUnit

JUnit has become the de facto standard when it comes to unit testing Java applications. The introduction of annotations in JUnit 4.x made it even easier to create tests and assert test results for expected values. JUnit can easily be integrated with build tools like ANT and Maven. It also has great tooling support available in all popular IDEs.

With JUnit, the standard practice is to write a separate class that holds test methods. This class is often referred to as a test case, and each test method is intended to test a single unit of work. It is also possible to organize test cases into groups referred to as test suites.

The best way to learn JUnit is to write a test method. Listing 4-1 shows a simple StringUtils class with an isEmpty method. The method takes a String as parameter and returns true if it is either null or an empty string.

Listing 4-1.

```
public class StringUtils {
    public static boolean isEmpty(String text) {
    return test == null || "".equals(test);
    }
}
```

Listing 4-2 is the JUnit class with a method to test the code.

Listing 4-2.

```
public class StringUtilsTest {
    @Test
    public void testIsEmpty() {
      Assert.assertTrue(StringUtils.isEmpty(null));
      Assert.assertTrue(StringUtils.isEmpty(""));
      Assert.assertFalse(StringUtils.isEmpty("Practical Spring Ldap"));
    }
}
```

Notice that I have followed the convention <Class Under Test>Test for naming the test class. Prior to JUnit 4.x, test methods needed to begin with the word "test". With 4.x, test methods just need to be marked with annotation @Test. Also notice that the testIsEmpty method holds several assertions for testing the isEmpty method's logic.

Table 4-1 lists some of the important annotations available in JUnit 4.

Table 4-1. *JUnit 4 Annotations*

Annotation	Description
@Test	Annotates a method as a JUnit test method. The method should be of public scope and have void return type.
@Before	Marks a method to run before every test method. Useful for setting up test fixtures. The @Before method of a superclass is run before the current class.
@After	Marks a method to be run after every test method. Useful for tearing down test fixtures. The @After method of a superclass is run before the current class.
@Ignore	Marks a method to be ignored during test runs. This helps avoid the need for commenting half-baked test methods.
@BeforeClass	Annotates a method to run before any test method is run. For a test case, the method is run only once and can be used to provide class level setup work.
@AfterClass	Annotates a method to run after all the test methods are run. This can be useful for performing any cleanups at a class level.
@RunWith	Specifies the class that is used to run the JUnit test case.

Testing Using Embedded LDAP Server

ApacheDS, OpenDJ, and UnboundID are open source LDAP directories that can be embedded into Java applications. Embedded directories are part of the application's JVM, making it easy to automate tasks such as startup and shutdown. They have a small startup time and typically run fast. Embedded directories also eliminate the need for a dedicated, standalone LDAP server for each developer or build machine.

■ **Note** Concepts discussed here serve as the foundation for the LdapUnit open source project. You will be using LdapUnit for testing code in all future chapters. Please visit http://ldapunit.org to download project artifacts and browse through the complete source code.

Embedding an LDAP server involves programmatically creating the server and starting/stopping it. However, despite their maturity, programmatically interacting with ApacheDS or OpenDJ is cumbersome. In the next section, you will look at the setup necessary to configure and use ApacheDS LDAP server.

Setting Up Embedded ApacheDS

Central to ApacheDS is the directory service that stores data and supports search operations. Thus, starting an ApacheDS LDAP server first involves creating and configuring a directory service. Listing 4-3 shows the code associated with creating a directory service. Note that you are simply using the DefaultDirectoryServiceFactory and initializing it.

Listing 4-3.

```
DirectoryServiceFactory dsf = DefaultDirectoryServiceFactory.DEFAULT;
dsf.init( "default" + UUID.randomUUID().toString() );
directoryService = dsf.getDirectoryService();
```

ApacheDS uses partitions to store LDAP entries. (A partition can be viewed as a logical container that holds an entire DIT). It is possible that a single ApacheDS instance can have multiple partitions. Associated with each partition is a root Distinguished Name (DN) called the partition suffix. All the entries in that partition are stored under that root DN. The code in Listing 4-4 creates a partition and adds it to the directoryService created in Listing 4-3.

Listing 4-4.

```
PartitionFactory partitionFactory =
     DefaultDirectoryServiceFactory.DEFAULT.getPartitionFactory();
/* Create Partition takes id, suffix, cache size, working directory*/
Partition partition = partitionFactory.createPartition("dc=inflinx,dc=com",
"dc=inflinx,dc=com", 1000, new File(
             directoryService.getWorkingDirectory(),rootDn));
partition.setSchemaManager(directoryService.getSchemaManager());

// Inject the partition into the DirectoryService
directoryService.addPartition( partition );
```

You create the partition using the partition factory. In order to create a new partition, you must provide the following information: a name that uniquely identifies the partition, a partition suffix or rootDn, cache size, and a working directory. In Listing 4-4, you have used the rootDn as the partition name also.

With the directory service created and configured, the next step is to create an LDAP server. Listing 4-5 shows the code associated with it. To the newly created LDAP Server, you provide a name. Then you create a TcpTransport object that will be listening on port 12389. The TcpTransport instance allows a client to communicate with your LDAP server.

Listing 4-5.

```
// Create the LDAP server
LdapServer ldapServer = new LdapServer();
ldapServer.setServiceName("Embedded LDAP service");
```

```
TcpTransport ldapTransport = new TcpTransport(12389);
ldapServer.setTransports(ldapTransport);
ldapServer.setDirectoryService( directoryService );
```

The final step is to start the service, which is achieved with the following code:

```
directoryService.startup();
ldapServer.start();
```

This completes the implementation of the startup method. The implementation of the shutdown method is described in Listing 4-6.

Listing 4-6.

```
public void stopServer() {
    try {
        System.out.println("Shutting down LDAP Server ....");
        ldapServer.stop();
        directoryService.shutdown();
        FileUtils.deleteDirectory( directoryService.getWorkingDirectory() );
        System.out.println("LDAP Server shutdown" + " successful ....");
    }
    catch(Exception e) {
        throw new RuntimeException(e);
    }
}
```

In addition to invoking the stop/shutdown method, notice that you have deleted the DirectoryService's working directory. The complete code for the embedded ApacheDS implementation is shown in Listing 4-7.

Listing 4-7.

```
package org.ldapunit.server;

import java.io.File;
import java.util.UUID;
import org.apache.commons.io.FileUtils;
import org.apache.directory.server.core.DirectoryService;
import org.apache.directory.server.core.factory.
DefaultDirectoryServiceFactory;
import org.apache.directory.server.core.factory. DirectoryServiceFactory;
import org.apache.directory.server.core.factory.PartitionFactory;
import org.apache.directory.server.core.partition.Partition;
import org.apache.directory.server.ldap.LdapServer;
import org.apache.directory.server.protocol.shared. transport.TcpTransport;
```

```java
public class ApacheDSConfigurer implements EmbeddedServerConfigurer {

    private DirectoryService directoryService;
    private LdapServer ldapServer;
    private String rootDn;
    private int port;

    public ApacheDSConfigurer(String rootDn, int port) {
        this.rootDn = rootDn;
        this.port = port;
    }

    public void startServer() {
        try {
            System.out.println("Starting Embedded " +
            "ApacheDS LDAP Server ....");
            DirectoryServiceFactory dsf = DefaultDirectoryServiceFactory.
            DEFAULT;
            dsf.init( "default" + UUID.randomUUID().toString());
            directoryService = dsf.getDirectoryService();

            PartitionFactory partitionFactory = DefaultDirectoryServiceFactory.
            DEFAULT.getPartitionFactory();

            /* Create Partition takes id, suffix, cache size, working
            directory*/
            Partition partition = partitionFactory.
            createPartition(rootDn,rootDn, 1000, new File(directoryService.
            getWorkingDirectory(), rootDn));
            partition.setSchemaManager(directoryService.getSchemaManager());

            // Inject the partition into the DirectoryService
            directoryService.addPartition( partition );

            // Create the LDAP server ldapServer = new LdapServer();
            ldapServer.setServiceName("Embedded LDAP service");
            TcpTransport ldapTransport = new TcpTransport(port);
            ldapServer.setTransports(ldapTransport);

            ldapServer.setDirectoryService( directoryService );
            directoryService.startup();
            ldapServer.start();

            System.out.println("Embedded ApacheDS LDAP server" + "has started
            successfully ....");
        }
```

```
        catch(Exception e) {
            throw new RuntimeException(e);
        }
    }

    public void stopServer() {
        try {
            System.out.println("Shutting down Embedded " + "ApacheDS LDAP
            Server ....");
            ldapServer.stop();
            directoryService.shutdown();
            FileUtils.deleteDirectory( directoryService.getWorkingDirectory() );

            System.out.println("Embedded ApacheDS LDAP " + "Server shutdown
            successful ....");
        }
        catch(Exception e) {
            throw new RuntimeException(e);
        }
    }
}
```

Creating Embedded Context Factory

With the above code in place, the next step is to automatically start the server and create contexts that you can use to interact with the embedded server. In Spring, you can achieve this by implementing a custom FactoryBean that creates new instances of ContextSource. In Listing 4-8, you start the creation of the context factory.

Listing 4-8.

```
package com.practicalspring.ldap.test;

import org.springframework.beans.factory.config. AbstractFactoryBean;
import org.springframework.ldap.core.ContextSource;
import org.springframework.ldap.core.support.DefaultDirObjectFactory;
import org.ldapunit.server.ApacheDSConfigurer;
import org.apache.directory.server.ldap.LdapServer;

public class EmbeddedContextSourceFactory extends
AbstractFactoryBean<ContextSource> {

    private int port;
    private String rootDn;
    private ApacheDSConfigurer apacheDsConfigurer;
```

```
@Override
public Class<?> getObjectType() {
    return ContextSource.class;
}

@Override
protected ContextSource createInstance() throws Exception {

    // To be implemented later.
    return null;
}
public void setRootDn(String rootDn) {
    this.rootDn = rootDn;
}
public void setPort(int port) {
    this.port = port;
}
}
```

Notice that the EmbeddedContextSourceFactory bean uses two setter methods: setPort and setRootDn. The setPort method can be used to set the port on which the embedded server should run. The setRootDn method can be used to provide the name of the root context. Listing 4-9 shows the implementation of the createInstance method, which creates a new instance of ApacheDSConfigurer and starts the server. Then it creates a new LdapContenxtSource and populates it with the embedded LDAP server information.

Listing 4-9.

```
apacheDsConfigurer = new ApacheDSConfigurer(rootDn, port);
apacheDsConfigurer.startServer();

LdapContextSource targetContextSource = new LdapContextSource();
targetContextSource.setUrl("ldap://localhost:" + port);
targetContextSource.setUserDn(ADMIN_DN);
targetContextSource.setPassword(ADMIN_PWD);
targetContextSource.setDirObjectFactory(DefaultDirObjectFactory.class);
targetContextSource.afterPropertiesSet();

return targetContextSource;
```

The implementation of destroyInstance is provided in Listing 4-10. It simply involves cleaning up the created context and stopping the embedded server.

Listing 4-10.

```java
@Override
protected void destroyInstance(ContextSource instance) throws Exception {
    super.destroyInstance(instance);
    apacheDsConfigurer.stopServer();
}
```

The final step is to create a Spring context file that uses the new context factory. This is shown in Listing 4-11. Notice that the embedded context source is being injected into the ldapTemplate.

Listing 4-11.

```xml
<?xml version="1.0" encoding="UTF-8"?>

<beans xmlns="http://www.springframework.org/schema/beans"
    xmlns:xsi="http://www.w3.org/2001/XMLSchema-instance"
    xmlns:context="http://www.springframework.org/schema/context"
    xsi:schemaLocation="http://www.springframework.org/schema/beans
    http://www.springframework.org/schema/beans/spring-beans.xsd
    http://www.springframework.org/schema/context
    http://www.springframework.org/schema/context/spring-context.xsd">

    <bean id="contextSource" class="com.inflinx.ldap.test.
    EmbeddedContextSourceFactory">
        <property name="port" value="12389" />
        <property name="rootDn" value="dc=inflinx,dc=com" />
    </bean>

    <bean id="ldapTemplate" class="org.springframework.ldap.core.
    LdapTemplate">
        <constructor-arg ref="contextSource" />
    </bean>
</beans>
```

Now you have the entire infrastructure needed to write JUnit test cases. Listing 4-12 shows a simple JUnit test case. This test case has a setup method that runs before each test method. In the setup method you load the data so that the LDAP server will be in a known state. In Listing 4-12, you are loading data from employees.ldif file. The teardown method runs after each test method is run. In the teardown method, you are deleting all the entries in LDAP server. This will allow you to start clean with a new test. The three test methods are very rudimentary and simply print the information on the console.

Listing 4-12.

```
package com.inflinx.book.ldap.test;

import java.util.List;

import org.junit.After;
import org.junit.Before;
import org.junit.Test;
import org.junit.runner.RunWith;

import org.springframework.beans.factory.annotation.Autowired;
import org.springframework.core.io.ClassPathResource;
import org.springframework.ldap.core.ContextMapper;
import org.springframework.ldap.core.ContextSource;
import org.springframework.ldap.core.DirContextAdapter;
import org.springframework.ldap.core.DistinguishedName;
import org.springframework.ldap.core.LdapTemplate;
import org.springframework.test.context.ContextConfiguration;
import org.springframework.test.context.junit4.SpringJUnit4ClassRunner;

@RunWith(SpringJUnit4ClassRunner.class )
@ContextConfiguration(locations= {"classpath:repositoryContext-test.xml"})
public class TestRepository {

    @Autowired
    ContextSource contextSource;

    @Autowired
    LdapTemplate ldapTemplate;

    @Before
    public void setup() throws Exception {
        System.out.println("Inside the setup");
        LdapUnitUtils.loadData(contextSource, new ClassPathResource
        ("employees.ldif"));
    }

    @After
    public void teardown() throws Exception {
        System.out.println("Inside the teardown");
        LdapUnitUtils.clearSubContexts(contextSource, new DistinguishedName
        ("dc=inflinx,dc=com"));
    }

    @Test
    public void testMethod() {
        System.out.println(getCount(ldapTemplate));
    }
```

```
@Test
public void testMethod2() {
    ldapTemplate.unbind(new DistinguishedName("uid=employee0,ou=employees,
    dc=inflinx,dc=com"));
    System.out.println(getCount(ldapTemplate));
}

@Test
public void testMethod3() {
    System.out.println(getCount(ldapTemplate));
}

private int getCount(LdapTemplate ldapTemplate) {
    List results = ldapTemplate.search("dc=inflinx,dc=com",
    "(objectClass=inetOrgPerson)", new ContextMapper() {
        @Override
        public Object mapFromContext(Object ctx) {
            return ((DirContextAdapter)ctx).getDn();
        }
    });
    return results.size();
}
}
```

Mocking LDAP Using EasyMock

In the previous section you looked at testing your LDAP code using an embedded LDAP
server. Now let's look at testing LDAP code using the EasyMock framework.

EasyMock is an open source library that makes creating and using mock objects
easy. Beginning with version 3.0, EasyMock natively supports mocking both interfaces
and concrete classes. The latest version of EasyMock can be downloaded from
http://easymock.org/Downloads.html. In order to mock concrete classes, two
additional libraries namely CGLIB and Objenesis are needed. Maven users can obtain
the required jar files by simply adding the following dependency in their pom.xml:

```
<dependency>
      <groupId>org.easymock</groupId>
      <artifactId>easymock</artifactId>
      <version>3.2</version>
      <scope>test</scope>
</dependency>
```

Creating a mock using EasyMock involves calling the createMock method on the EasyMock class. The following example creates a mock object for LdapTemplate:

```
LdapTemplate ldapTemplate = EasyMock.createMock(LdapTemplate. class);
```

Each newly created mock object starts in the recording mode. In this mode you record the expected behavior or expectation of the mock. For example, you can tell the mock that if this method gets called, return this value. For example, the following code adds a new expectation to the LdapTemplate mock:

```
EasyMock.expect(ldapTemplate.bind(isA(DirContextOperations. class)));
```

In this code you are instructing the mock that a bind method will be invoked and an instance of DirContextOperations will be passed in as its parameter.

Once all the expectations are recorded, the mock needs to be able to replay these expectations. This is done by invoking the replay method on EasyMock and passing in the mock objects that needs to be replayed as parameters.

```
EasyMock.replay(ldapTemplate);
```

The mock object can now be used in test cases. Once the code under test completes its execution, you can verify if all the expectations on the mock are met. This is done by invoking the verify method on EasyMock.

```
EasyMock.verify(ldapTemplate);
```

Mocking can be especially useful for verifying context row mappers used in the search methods. As you have seen before, a row mapper implementation converts an LDAP context/entry into a Java domain object. Here is the method signature in the ContextMapper interface that performs the conversion:

```
public Object mapFromContext(Object ctx)
```

The ctx parameter in this method will typically be an instance of the DirContextOperations implementation. So, in order to unit test ContextMapper implementations, you need to pass in a mock DirContextOperations instance to the mapFromContext method. The mock DirContextOperations should return dummy but valid data so that the ContextMapper implementation can create a domain object from it. Listing 4-13 shows the code to mock and populate a DirContextOperations instance. The mockContextOperations loops through the passed-in dummy attribute data and adds expectations for single- and multi-valued attributes.

Listing 4-13.

```
public static DirContextOperations mockContextOperations(Map<String, Object>
attributes) {

    DirContextOperations contextOperations = createMock(DirContextOperations.
    class);
        for(Entry<String, Object> entry : attributes.entrySet()){
            if(entry.getValue() instanceof String){
                expect(contextOperations.getStringAttribute(eq(entry.
                getKey()))).andReturn((String)entry.getValue());
                expectLastCall().anyTimes();
            }
            else if(entry.getValue() instanceof String[]){
                expect(contextOperations.
                getStringAttributes(eq(entry.getKey()))).andReturn((String[])
                entry.getValue());
                expectLastCall().anyTimes();
            }
        }
    return contextOperations;
}
```

With this code in place, Listing 4-14 shows the code that uses the
mockContextOperations method for mock testing context row mapper.

Listing 4-14.

```
public class ContextMapperExample {

    @Test
    public void testConextMapper() {
        Map<String, Object> attributes = new HashMap<String, Object>();
        attributes.put("uid", "employee1");
        attributes.put("givenName", "John"); attributes.put("surname", "Doe");
        attributes.put("telephoneNumber", new String[]
        {"8011001000","8011001001"});

        DirContextOperations contextOperations = LdapMockUtils.
        mockContextOperations(attributes);
        replay(contextOperations);

        //Now we can use the context operations to test a mapper
        EmployeeContextMapper mapper = new EmployeeContextMapper();
        Employee employee = (Employee)mapper.mapFromContext(contextOperations);
        verify(contextOperations);
```

```
    // test the employee object
    assertEquals(employee.getUid(), "employee1");
    assertEquals(employee.getFirstName(), "John");
  }
}
```

Test Data Generation

For testing purposes, you often need to generate initial test data. OpenDJ provides a great command-line utility called make- ldif that makes generating test LDAP data a breeze. Please refer to Chapter 3 for instructions on installing OpenDJ. The command-line tools for Windows OS are located in the bat folder under the OpenDJ installation.

The make-ldif tool requires a template for creating test data. You will use the patron.template file shown in Listing 4-15 for generating patron entries.

Listing 4-15.

```
define suffix=dc=inflinx,dc=com
define maildomain=inflinx.com
define numusers=101

branch: [suffix]

branch: ou=patrons,[suffix]
subordinateTemplate: person:[numusers]

template: person
rdnAttr: uid
objectClass: top
objectClass: person
objectClass: organizationalPerson
objectClass: inetOrgPerson
givenName: <first>
sn: <last>
cn: {givenName} {sn}
initials: {givenName:1}<random:chars:ABCDEFGHIJKLMNOPQRSTUVWXYZ:1>{sn:1}
employeeNumber: <sequential:0>
uid: patron<sequential:0>
mail: {uid}@[maildomain]
userPassword: password
telephoneNumber: <random:telephone>
homePhone: <random:telephone>
mobile: <random:telephone>
street: <random:numeric:5> <file:streets> Street
l: <file:cities>
```

```
st: <file:states>
postalCode: <random:numeric:5>
postalAddress: {cn}${street}${l}, {st} {postalCode}
```

This is a simple modification to the example.template file that comes out of the box with the installation. The example.template is located in <OpenDJ_Install>\config\ MakeLDIF folder. The uid has been modified to use the prefix "patron" instead of "user". Also, the numUsers value has been changed to 101. This indicates the number of test users you would like the script to generate. To generate the test data, run the following command in a command line:

```
C:\ practicalldap\opendj\bat>make-ldif --ldifFile
c:\ practicalldap\testdata\patrons.ldif --templateFile
c:\ practicalldap\templates\patron.template --randomSeed 1
```

- The --ldifFile option is used to specify the target file location. Here you are storing it under the name patrons.ldif in the testdata directory

- The --templateFile is used to specify the template file to be used.

- The --randomSeed is an integer that needs to be used to seed the random number generator used during data generation.

Upon successful creation, you will see a screen similar to Figure 4-1. In addition to the 101 test entries, the script creates two additional base entries.

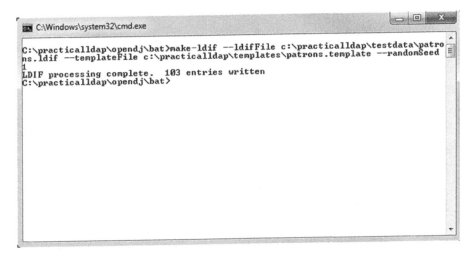

Figure 4-1. Make LDIF command result

Summary

In this chapter, you took a deep dive into testing LDAP code. You started with an overview of testing concepts. Then you spent time setting up ApacheDS for embedded testing. Although embedded testing simplifies things, there are times where you want to test code, minimizing the need for external infrastructure dependencies. You can address those situations using mock testing. Finally, you used OpenDJ tools to generate test data.

In the next chapter, you will look at creating Data Access Objects (DAOs) that interact with LDAP using object factories.

CHAPTER 5

■ ■ ■

Advanced Spring LDAP

In this chapter, you will learn

- The basics of JNDI object factories.
- DAO implementation using object factories.

JNDI Object Factories

JNDI provides the notion of object factories, which makes dealing with LDAP information easier. As the name suggests, an object factory transforms directory information into objects that are meaningful to the application. For example, using object factories it is possible to have a search operation return object instances like `Patron` or `Employee` instead of plain `javax.naming.NamingEnumeration`.

Figure 5-1 depicts the flow involved when an application performs LDAP operations in conjunction with an object factory. The flow starts with the application invoking a search or a lookup operation. The JNDI API will execute the requested operation and retrieves entries from LDAP. These results are then passed over to the registered object factory, which transforms them into objects. These objects are handed over to the application.

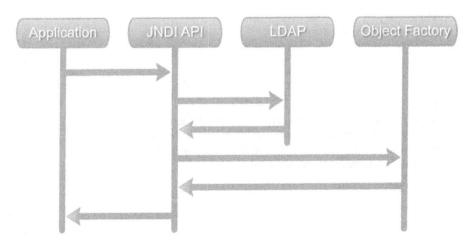

Figure 5-1. *JNDI/object factory flow*

Object factories dealing with LDAP need to implement the javax.naming.spi.
DirObjectFactory interface. Listing 5-1 shows a Patron object factory implementation
that takes the passed-in information and creates a Patron instance. The obj parameter to
the getObjectInstance method holds reference information about the object. The name
parameter holds the name of the object. The attrs parameter contains the attributes
associated with the object. In the getObjectInstance you read the required attributes
and populate the newly created Patron instance.

Listing 5-1.

```
package com.inflinx.book.ldap;

import java.util.Hashtable;
import javax.naming.Context;
import javax.naming.Name;
import javax.naming.directory.Attributes;
import javax.naming.directory.BasicAttributes;
import javax.naming.spi.DirObjectFactory
import com.inflinx.book.ldap.domain.Patron;

public class PatronObjectFactory implements DirObjectFactory {

    @Override
    public Object getObjectInstance(Object obj, Name name, Context
    nameCtx,Hashtable<?, ?> environment, Attributes attrs) throws Exception {
        Patron patron = new Patron();
        patron.setUid(attrs.get("uid").toString());
        patron.setFullName(attrs.get("cn").toString());
        return patron;
    }

    @Override
    public Object getObjectInstance(Object obj, Name name, Context
    nameCtx,Hashtable<?, ?> environment) throws Exception {
        return getObjectInstance(obj, name, nameCtx, environment,
        new BasicAttributes());
    }
}
```

Before you can start using this object factory, it must be registered during Initial Context
creation. Listing 5-2 shows an example of using PatronObjectFactory during lookups. You
register the PatronObjectFactory class using the DirContext.OBJECT_FACTORIES property.
Notice that the context's lookup method now returns a Patron instance.

Listing 5-2.

```java
package com.inflinx.book.ldap;

import java.util.Properties;
import javax.naming.NamingException;
import javax.naming.directory.DirContext;
import javax.naming.ldap.InitialLdapContext;
import javax.naming.ldap.LdapContext;
import com.inflinx.book.ldap.domain.Patron;

public class JndiObjectFactoryLookupExample {

    private LdapContext getContext() throws NamingException {
        Properties environment = new Properties();
        environment.setProperty(DirContext.INITIAL_CONTEXT_FACTORY,
        "com.sun.jndi.ldap.LdapCtxFactory");
        environment.setProperty(DirContext.PROVIDER_URL,
        "ldap://localhost:11389");
        environment.setProperty(DirContext.SECURITY_PRINCIPAL,
        "cn=Directory Manager");
        environment.setProperty(DirContext.SECURITY_CREDENTIALS, "opends");
        environment.setProperty(DirContext.OBJECT_FACTORIES,
        "com.inflinx.book.ldap.PatronObjectFactory");

            return new InitialLdapContext(environment, null);
    }

    public Patron lookupPatron(String dn) {
        Patron patron = null;
        try {
            LdapContext context = getContext();
            patron = (Patron) context.lookup(dn);
        }
        catch(NamingException e) {
          e.printStackTrace();
        }
        return patron;
    }

    public static void main(String[] args) {
        JndiObjectFactoryLookupExample jle = new JndiObjectFactoryLookupExample();
        Patron p = jle.lookupPatron("uid=patron99,ou=patrons,"
        + "dc=inflinx,dc=com");
        System.out.println(p);
        }
}
```

Spring and Object Factories

Spring LDAP provides an out-of-the-box implementation of DirObjectFactory called org.springframework.ldap.core.support.DefaultDirObjectFactory. As you saw in the previous section, the PatronObjectFactory creates instances of Patrons from the contexts found. Similarly, the DefaultDirObjectFactory creates instances of org.springframework.ldap.core.DirContextAdapter from found contexts.

The DirContextAdapter class is generic in nature and can be viewed as a holder of LDAP entry data. The DirContextAdapter class provides a variety of utility methods that greatly simplify getting and setting attributes. As you will see in later sections, when changes are made to attributes, the DirContextAdapter automatically keeps track of those changes and simplifies updating LDAP entry's data. The simplicity of the DirContextAdapter along with DefaultDirObjectFactory enables you to easily convert LDAP data into domain objects, reducing the need to write and register a lot of object factories.

In the next sections, you will be using the DirContextAdapter to create an Employee DAO that abstracts read and write access of Employee LDAP entries.

DAO DESIGN PATTERN

Most Java and JEE applications today access a persistent store of some type for their everyday activities. The persistent stores vary from popular relational databases to LDAP directories to legacy mainframe systems. Depending on the type of persistent store, the mechanism to obtain and manipulate data will vary greatly. This can result in tight coupling between the application and data access code, making it hard to switch between the implementations. This is where a Data Access Object or DAO pattern can help.

The Data Access Object is a popular core JEE pattern that encapsulates access to data sources. Low-level data access logic such as connecting to the data source and manipulating data is cleanly abstracted to a separate layer by the DAO. A DAO implementation usually includes the following:

1. A DAO interface that provides the CRUD method contract.

2. Concrete implementation of the interface using a data source-specific API.

3. Domain objects or transfer objects that are returned by the DAO.

With a DAO in place, the rest of the application need not worry about the underlying data implementation and can focus on high-level business logic.

DAO Implementation Using Object Factory

Typically the DAOs you create in Spring applications have an interface that serves as the DAO's contract and an implementation that contains the actual logic to access the data store or directory. Listing 5-3 shows the EmployeeDao interface for the Employee DAO you will be implementing. The DAO has create, update, and delete methods for modifying the employee information. It also has two finder methods, one that retrieves an employee by its id and another that returns all the employees.

Listing 5-3.

```
package com.inflinx.book.ldap.repository;
import java.util.List;
import com.inflinx.book.ldap.domain.Employee;
public interface EmployeeDao {
    public void create(Employee employee);
    public void update(Employee employee);
    public void delete(String id);
    public Employee find(String id);
    public List<Employee> findAll();
}
```

The previous EmployeeDao interface uses an Employee domain object. Listing 5-4 shows this Employee domain object. The Employee implementation holds all the important attributes of a Library employee. Notice that instead of using the fully qualified DN, you will be using the uid attribute as the object's unique identifier.

Listing 5-4.

```
package com.inflinx.book.ldap.domain;
public class Employee {
    private String uid;
    private String firstName;
    private String lastName;
    private String commonName;
    private String email;
    private int departmentNumber;
    private String employeeNumber;
    private String[] phone;
    // getters and setters omitted for brevity
}
```

You start with a basic implementation of the EmployeeDao, as shown in Listing 5-5.

Listing 5-5.

```
package com.inflinx.book.ldap.repository;

import java.util.List;
import org.springframework.beans.factory.annotation.Autowired;
import org.springframework.beans.factory.annotation.Qualifier;
import org.springframework.ldap.core.simple.SimpleLdapTemplate;
import com.practicalspring.springldap.domain.Employee;

@Repository("employeeDao" )
public class EmployeeDaoLdapImpl implements EmployeeDao {

    @Autowired
    @Qualifier("ldapTemplate" )
    private SimpleLdapTemplate ldapTemplate;

    @Override
    public List<Employee> findAll() { return null; }

    @Override
    public Employee find(String id) { return null; }

    @Override
    public void create(Employee employee) {}

    @Override
    public void delete(String id) {}

    @Override
    public void update(Employee employee) {}

}
```

In this implementation, you are injecting an instance of SimpleLdapTemplate. The actual creation of the SimpleLdapTemplate will be done in an external configuration file. Listing 5-6 shows the repositoryContext.xml file with SimpleLdapTemplate and associated bean declarations.

Listing 5-6.

```
<?xml version="1.0" encoding="UTF-8"?>

<beans xmlns="http://www.springframework.org/schema/beans"
xmlns:xsi="http://www.w3.org/2001/XMLSchema-instance"
xmlns:context="http://www.springframework.org/schema/context"
xsi:schemaLocation="http://www.springframework.org/schema/beans
http://www.springframework.org/schema/beans/spring-beans.xsd
```

```
http://www.springframework.org/schema/context
http://www.springframework.org/schema/context/spring-context.xsd ">

    <context:component-scan base-package="com.inflinx.book.ldap" />

    <bean id="contextSource" class=
    "org.springframework.ldap.core.support.LdapContextSource">
        <property name="url" value="ldap://localhost:11389" />
        <property name="base" value="ou=employees,dc=inflinx,dc=com"/>
        <property name="userDn" value="uid=admin,ou=system" />
        <property name="password" value="secret" />
    </bean>
    <bean id="ldapTemplate" class=
    "org.springframework.ldap.core.simple.SimpleLdapTemplate">
        <constructor-arg ref="contextSource" />
    </bean>
</beans>
```

This configuration file is similar to the one you saw in Chapter 3. You provide the
LDAP server information to the LdapContextSource to create a contextSource bean.
By setting the base to "ou=employees,dc=inflinx,dc=com", you have restricted all the
LDAP operations to the employee branch of the LDAP tree. It is important to understand
that a search operation on the branch "ou=patrons" will not be possible using the
contexts created here. If the requirement is to search all of the branches of the LDAP tree,
then the base property needs to be an empty string.

An important property of LdapContextSource is the dirObjectFactory, which
can be used to set a DirObjectFactory to use. However, in Listing 5-6, you didn't
use this property to specify your intent to use DefaultDirObjectFactory. That is
because by default LdapContextSource registers the DefaultDirObjectFactory as its
DirObjectFactory.

In the final portion of the configuration file you have the SimpleLdapTemplate
bean declaration. You have passed in the LdapContextSource bean as the constructor
argument to the SimpleLdapTemplate.

Implementing Finder Methods

Implementing the findAll method of the Employee DAO requires searching LDAP for
all the employee entries and creating Employee instances with the returned entries. To do
this, you will be using the following method in the SimpleLdapTemplate class:

```
public <T> List<T> search(String base, String filter,
ParameterizedContextMapper<T> mapper)
```

Since you are using the DefaultDirObjectFactory, every time a search or a lookup is performed, every context found in the LDAP tree will be returned as an instance of DirContextAdapter. Like the search method you saw in Listing 3-8, the above search method takes a base and filter parameters. Additionally, it takes an instance of ParameterizedContextMapper<T>. The above search method will pass the returned DirContextAdapters to the ParameterizedContextMapper<T> instance for transformation.

The ParameterizedContextMapper<T> and its parent interface, the ContextMapper, hold the mapping logic needed to populate domain objects from the passed-in DirContextAdapter. Listing 5-7 provides the context mapper implementation for mapping Employee instances. As you can see, the EmployeeContextMapper extends AbstractParameterizedContextMapper, which is an abstract class that implements ParameterizedContextMapper.

Listing 5-7.

```java
package com.inflinx.book.ldap.repository.mapper;

import org.springframework.ldap.core.DirContextOperations;
import org.springframework.ldap.core.simple.
AbstractParameterizedContextMapper;
import com.inflinx.book.ldap.domain.Employee;

public class EmployeeContextMapper
extends AbstractParameterizedContextMapper<Employee> {

    @Override
    protected Employee doMapFromContext(DirContextOperations context) {

    Employee employee = new Employee();
    employee.setUid(context.getStringAttribute("UID"));
    employee.setFirstName(context.getStringAttribute("givenName"));
    employee.setLastName(context.getStringAttribute("surname"));
    employee.setCommonName(context.getStringAttribute("commonName"));
    employee.setEmployeeNumber(context.getStringAttribute("employeeNumber"));
    employee.setEmail(context.getStringAttribute("mail"));
    employee.setDepartmentNumber(Integer.parseInt(context.getStringAttribute
    ("departmentNumber")));
    employee.setPhone(context.getStringAttributes("telephoneNumber"));

    return employee;
    }
}
```

In Listing 5-7, the DirContextOperations parameter to the doMapFromContext method is an interface for DirContextAdapter. As you can see, the doMapFromContext implementation involves creating a new Employee instance and reading the attributes you are interested in from the supplied context.

With the EmployeeContextMapper in place, the findAll method implementation becomes trivial. Since all the employee entries have the objectClass inetOrgPerson, you will be using "(objectClass=inetOrgPerson)" as the search filter. Listing 5-8 shows the findAll implementation.

Listing 5-8.

```
@Override
public List<Employee> findAll() {
    return ldapTemplate.search("", "(objectClass=inetOrgPerson)",
    new EmployeeContextMapper());
}
```

The other finder method can be implemented in two ways: searching an LDAP tree with the filter (uid=<supplied employee id>) or performing an LDAP lookup with an employee DN. Since search operations with filters are more expensive than looking up a DN, you will be implementing the find method using the lookup. Listing 5-9 shows the find method implementation.

Listing 5-9.

```
@Override
public Employee find(String id) {
    DistinguishedName dn = new DistinguishedName();
    dn.add("uid", id);
    return ldapTemplate.lookup(dn, new EmployeeContextMapper());
}
```

You start the implementation by constructing a DN for the employee. Since the initial context base is restricted to the employee branch, you have just specified the RDN portion of the employee entry. Then you use the lookup method to look up the employee entry and create an Employee instance using the EmployeeContextMapper.

This concludes the implementation of both finder methods. Let's create a JUnit test class for testing your finder methods. The test case is shown in Listing 5-10.

Listing 5-10.

```
package com.inflinx.book.ldap.repository;

import java.util.List;
import org.junit.After;
import org.junit.Assert;
import org.junit.Before;
import org.junit.Test;
```

```java
import org.junit.runner.RunWith;
import org.ldapunit.util.LdapUnitUtils;
import org.springframework.beans.factory.annotation.Autowired;
import org.springframework.beans.factory.annotation.Qualifier;
import org.springframework.core.io.ClassPathResource;
import org.springframework.ldap.core.DistinguishedName;
import org.springframework.test.context.ContextConfiguration;
import org.springframework.test.context.junit4.SpringJUnit4ClassRunner;
import com.inflinx.book.ldap.domain.Employee;

@RunWith(SpringJUnit4ClassRunner.class )
@ContextConfiguration(locations={"classpath:repositoryContext-test.xml"})
public class EmployeeDaoLdapImplTest {

    private static final String PORT = "12389";
    private static final String ROOT_DN = "dc=inflinx,dc=com";

    @Autowired
    @Qualifier("employeeDao" )
    private EmployeeDao employeeDao;

    @Before
    public void setup() throws Exception {
        System.out.println("Inside the setup");
        LdapUnitUtils.loadData(new ClassPathResource("employees.ldif"), PORT);
    }

    @After
    public void teardown() throws Exception {
        System.out.println("Inside the teardown");
        LdapUnitUtils.clearSubContexts(new DistinguishedName(ROOT_DN), PORT);
    }

    @Test
    public void testFindAll() {
        List<Employee> employeeList = employeeDao.findAll();
        Assert.assertTrue(employeeList.size() > 0);
    }

    @Test
    public void testFind() {
        Employee employee = employeeDao.find("employee1");
        Assert.assertNotNull(employee);
    }
}
```

Notice that you have specified the repositoryContext-test.xml in the ContextConfiguration. This test context file is shown in Listing 5-11. In the configuration file you have created an embedded context source using the LdapUnit framework's EmbeddedContextSourceFactory class. The embedded LDAP server is an instance of OpenDJ (as specified by the property serverType) and will run on port 12389.

The setup and teardown methods in the JUnit test case are implemented for loading and deleting test employee data. The employee.ldif file contains the test data you will be using throughout this book.

Listing 5-11.

```xml
<?xml version="1.0" encoding="UTF-8"?>

<beans xmlns="http://www.springframework.org/schema/beans"
xmlns:xsi="http://www.w3.org/2001/XMLSchema-instance"
xmlns:context="http://www.springframework.org/schema/context"
xsi:schemaLocation="http://www.springframework.org/schema/beans
http://www.springframework.org/schema/beans/spring-beans.xsd
http://www.springframework.org/schema/context
http://www.springframework.org/schema/context/spring-context.xsd">

    <context:component-scan base-package="com.inflinx.book.ldap" />

    <bean id="contextSource" class=
    "org.ldapunit.context.EmbeddedContextSourceFactory">
        <property name="port" value="12389" />
        <property name="rootDn" value="dc=inflinx,dc=com" />
        <property name="base" value="ou=employees,dc=inflinx,dc=com" />
        <property name="serverType" value="OPENDJ" />
    </bean>
    <bean id="ldapTemplate" class=
    "org.springframework.ldap.core.simple.SimpleLdapTemplate">
        <constructor-arg ref="contextSource" />
    </bean>
</beans>
```

Create Method

SimpleLdapTemplate provides several bind methods for adding entries to LDAP. To create a new Employee you will use the following bind method variation:

```
public void bind(DirContextOperations ctx)
```

This method takes a DirContextOperations instance as its parameter. The bind method invokes the getDn method on the passed-in DirContextOperations instance and retrieves the fully qualified DN of the entry. It then binds all the attributes to the DN and creates a new entry.

The implementation of the create method in the Employee DAO is shown in Listing 5-12. As you can see, you start by creating a new instance of a DirContextAdapter. Then you populate the context's attributes with employee information. Notice that the departmentNumber's int value is being explicitly converted to a String. If this conversion is not done, the method will end up throwing an "org.springframework. ldap.InvalidAttributeValueException" exception. The last line in the method does the actual binding.

Listing 5-12.

```
@Override
public void create(Employee employee) {

    DistinguishedName dn = new DistinguishedName();
    dn.add("uid", employee.getUid());
    DirContextAdapter context = new DirContextAdapter();
    context.setDn(dn);
    context.setAttributeValues("objectClass", new String[]
    {"top", "person", "organizationalPerson", "inetOrgPerson"});
    context.setAttributeValue("givenName", employee.getFirstName());
    context.setAttributeValue("surname", employee.getLastName());
    context.setAttributeValue("commonName", employee.getCommonName());
    context.setAttributeValue("mail", employee.getEmail());
    context.setAttributeValue("departmentNumber",
    Integer.toString(employee.getDepartmentNumber()));
    context.setAttributeValue("employeeNumber",
    employee.getEmployeeNumber());
    context.setAttributeValues("telephoneNumber",employee.getPhone());

    ldapTemplate.bind(context);
}
```

■ **Note**   Compare the code in Listing 5-12 with the code in Listing 3-10. You can clearly see that DirContextAdapter does a great job simplifying attribute manipulation.

Let's quickly verify the create method's implementation with the JUnit test case in Listing 5-13.

Listing 5-13.

```
@Test
public void testCreate() {
    Employee employee = new Employee();
    employee.setUid("employee1000");
    employee.setFirstName("Test");
    employee.setLastName("Employee1000");
```

```
employee.setCommonName("Test Employee1000");
employee.setEmail("employee1000@inflinx.com" );
employee.setDepartmentNumber(12356);
employee.setEmployeeNumber("45678");
employee.setPhone(new String[]{"801-100-1200"});

employeeDao.create(employee);
}
```

Update Method

Updating an entry involves adding, replacing, or removing its attributes. The simplest way to achieve this is to remove the entire entry and create it with a new set of attributes. This technique is referred to as rebinding. Deleting and recreating an entry is obviously not efficient, and it makes more sense to just operate on changed values.

In Chapter 3, you used the modifyAttributes and ModificationItem instances for updating LDAP entries. Even though modifyAttributes is a nice approach, it does require a lot of work to manually generate the ModificationItem list. Thankfully, DirContextAdapter automates this and makes updating an entry a breeze. Listing 5-14 shows the update method implementation using DirContextAdapter.

Listing 5-14.

```
@Override
public void update(Employee employee) {
    DistinguishedName dn = new DistinguishedName();
    dn.add("uid", employee.getUid());

    DirContextOperations context = ldapTemplate.lookupContext(dn);
    context.setAttributeValues("objectClass", new String[] {"top", "person",
    "organizationalPerson", "inetOrgPerson"});
    context.setAttributeValue("givenName", employee.getFirstName());
    context.setAttributeValue("surname", employee.getLastName());
    context.setAttributeValue("commonName", employee.getCommonName());
    context.setAttributeValue("mail", employee.getEmail());
    context.setAttributeValue("departmentNumber",
    Integer.toString(employee.getDepartmentNumber()));
    context.setAttributeValue("employeeNumber",
    employee.getEmployeeNumber());
    context.setAttributeValues("telephoneNumber", employee.getPhone());

    ldapTemplate.modifyAttributes(context);
}
```

In this implementation, you will notice that you first look up the existing context using the employee's DN. Then you set all the attributes like you did in the create method. (The difference being that DirContextAdapter keeps track of value changes made to the entry.) Finally, you pass in the updated context to the modifyAttributes method. The modifyAttributes method will retrieve the modified items list from the DirContextAdapter and perform those modifications on the entry in LDAP. Listing 5-15 shows the associated test case that updates the first name of an employee.

Listing 5-15.

```
@Test
public void testUpdate() {
    Employee employee1 = employeeDao.find("employee1");
    employee1.setFirstName("Employee New");
    employeeDao.update(employee1);
    employee1 = employeeDao.find("employee1");
    Assert.assertEquals(employee1.getFirstName(),"Employee New");
}
```

Delete Method

Spring LDAP makes unbinding straightforward with the unbind method in the LdapTemplate/SimpleLdapTemplate. Listing 5-16 shows the code involved in deleting an employee.

Listing 5-16.

```
@Override
public void delete(String id) {
    DistinguishedName dn = new DistinguishedName();
    dn.add("uid", id);
    ldapTemplate.unbind(dn);
}
```

Since your operations are all relative to the initial context with the base "ou=employees,dc=inflinx,dc=com", you create the DN with just uid, the entry's RDN. Invoking the unbind operation will remove the entry and all its associated attributes.

Listing 5-17 shows the associated test case to verify the deletion of the entry. Once an entry is successfully removed, any find operation on that name will result in a NameNotFoundException. The test case validates this assumption.

Listing 5-17.

```
@Test(expected=org.springframework.ldap.NameNotFoundException.class)
public void testDelete() {
    String empUid = "employee11";
    employeeDao.delete(empUid);
    employeeDao.find(empUid);
}
```

Summary

In this chapter, you were introduced to the world of JNDI object factories. You then looked at the DefaultDirObjectFactory, Spring LDAP's object factory implementation. You spent the rest of the chapter implementing an Employee DAO using DirContextAdapter and SimpleLdapTemplate.

In the next chapter, you will take a deep dive into the world of LDAP search and search filters.

■ ■ ■

## CHAPTER 6

Searching LDAP

In this chapter you will learn

- The basics of LDAP search
- LDAP search using filters
- Creating custom search filter

Searching for information is the most common operation performed against LDAP. A client application initiates an LDAP search by passing in search criteria, the information that determines where to search and what to search for. Upon receiving the request, the LDAP server executes the search and returns all the entries that match the criteria.

LDAP Search Criteria

The LDAP search criteria are made up of three mandatory parameters—base, scope, and filter and several optional parameters. Let's look at each of these parameters in detail.

Base Parameter

The base portion of the search is a Distinguished Name (DN) that identifies the branch of the tree that will be searched. For example, a base of "ou=patrons, dc=inflinx, dc=com" indicates that the search will start in the Patron branch and move downwards. It is also possible to specify an empty base, which will result in searching the root DSE entry.

■ **Note** The root DSE or DSA-Specific Entry is a special entry in the LDAP server. It typically holds server-specific data such as the vendor name, vendor version, and different controls and features that it supports.

Scope Parameter

The scope parameter determines how deep, relative to the base, an LDAP search needs to be performed. LDAP protocol defines three possible search scopes: base, one level, and subtree. Figure 6-1 illustrates the entries that get evaluated as part of the search with different scopes.

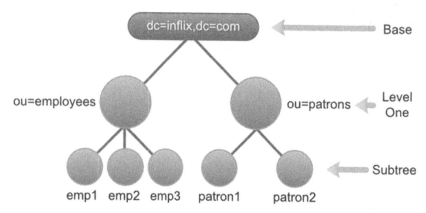

Figure 6-1. *Search scopes*

The base scope restricts the search to the LDAP entry identified by the base parameter. No other entries will be included as part of the search. In your Library application schema, with a base DN `dc=inflinx,dc=com` and scope of base, a search would just return the root organization entry, as shown in Figure 6-1.

The one level scope indicates searching all the entries one level directly below the base. The base entry itself is not included in the search. So, with base `dc=inflinx,dc=com` and scope one level, a search for all entries would return employees and patrons organizational unit.

Finally, the subtree scope includes the base entry and all of its descendent entries in the search. This is the slowest and most expensive option of the three. In your Library example, a search with this scope and base `dc=inflinx, dc=com` would return all the entries.

Filter Parameter

In your Library application LDAP Server, let's say you want to find all the patrons that live in the Midvale area. From the LDAP schema, you know that patron entries have the `city` attribute that holds the city name they live in. So this requirement essentially boils down to retrieving all entries that have the `city` attribute with a value of "Midvale". This is exactly what a search filter does. A search filter defines the characteristics that all the returning entries possess. Logically speaking, the filter gets applied to each entry in the set identified by base and scope. Only the entries that match the filter become part of the returned search results.

An LDAP search filter is made up of three components: an attribute type, an operator, and a value (or range of values) for the attribute. Depending on the operator, the value part can be optional. These components must always be enclosed inside parentheses, like so:

```
Filter = (attributetype operator value)
```

With this information in hand, the search filter to locate all patrons living in Midvale would look like this:

```
(city=Midvale)
```

Now, let's say you want to find all the patrons who live in Midvale area *and* have an e-mail address so that you can send them news of occasional library events. The resulting search filter is essentially a combination of two filter items: an item that identifies patrons in the city of Midvale and an item that identifies patrons that have an e-mail address. You have already seen the first item of the filter. Here is the other portion of the filter:

```
(mail=*)
```

The =* operator indicates the presence of an attribute. So the expression mail=* will return all entries that have a value in their mail attribute. The LDAP specification defines filter operators that can be used to combine multiple filters and create complex filters. Here is the format for combining the filters:

```
Filter = (operator filter1 filter2)
```

Notice the use of prefix notation, where the operator is written before their operands for combining the two filters. Here is the required filter for your use case:

```
(&(city=Midvale)(mail=*))
```

The & in this filter is an *And* operator. The LDAP specification defines a variety of search filter operators. Table 6-1 lists some of the commonly used operators.

Table 6-1. Search Filter Operators

Name	Symbol	Example	Description
Equality Filter	=	(sn=Smith)	Matches all the entries with last name Smith.
Substring Filter	=, *	(sn=Smi*)	Matches all entries whose last name begins with Smi.
Greater Than or Equals Filter	>=	(sn>=S*)	Matches all entries that are alphabetically greater than or equal to S.

(continued)

Table 6-1. (*continued*)

Name	Symbol	Example	Description
Less Than or Equals Filter	<=	(sn<=S*)	Matches all entries that are alphabetically lower than or equals to S.
Presence Filter	=*	(objectClass=*)	Matches all entries that have the attribute objectClass. This is a popular expression used to retrieve all entries in LDAP.
Approximate Filter	~=	(sn~=Smith)	Matches all entries whose last name is a variation of Smith. So this can return Smith and Snith.
And Filter	&	(&(sn=Smith) (zip=84121))	Returns all Smiths living in the 84121 area.
Or Filter	|	(|(sn=Smith) (sn=Lee))	Returns all entries with last name Smith or Lee.
Not Filter	!	(!(sn=Smith))	Returns all entries whose last name is not Smith.

Optional Parameters

In addition to the above three parameters, it is possible to include several optional parameters to control search behavior. For example, the timelimit parameter indicates the time allowed to complete the search. Similarly, the sizelimit parameter places an upper bound on the number of entries that can be returned as part of the result.

A very commonly used optional parameter involves providing a list of attribute names. When a search is performed, the LDAP server by default returns all the attributes associated with entries found in the search. Sometimes this might not be desirable. In those scenarios, you can provide a list of attribute names as part of the search, and the LDAP server would return only entries with those attributes. Here is an example of search method in the LdapTemplate that takes an array of attribute names (ATTR_1, ATTR_2, and ATTR_3):

```
ldapTemplate.search("SEARCH_BASE", "uid=USER_DN", 1, new String[]{"ATTR_1",
"ATTR_2", ATTR_3}, new SomeContextMapperImpl());
```

When this search is performed, the entries returned will only have ATTR_1, ATTR_2, and ATTR_3. This could reduce the amount of data transferred from the server and is useful in high traffic situations.

Since version 3, LDAP servers can maintain attributes for each entry for purely administrative purposes. These attributes are referred to as operational attributes and are not part of the entry's objectClass. When an LDAP search is performed, the returned entries will not contain the operational attributes by default. In order to retrieve operational attributes, you need to provide a list of operational attributes names in the search criteria.

■ **Note**   Examples of operational attributes include `createTimeStamp`, which holds the time when the entry was created, and `pwdAccountLockedTime`, which records the time when a user's account was locked.

LDAP INJECTION

LDAP injection is a technique where an attacker alters an LDAP query to run arbitrary LDAP statements against the directory server. LDAP injection can result in unauthorized data access or modifications to the LDAP tree. Applications that don't perform proper input validation or sanitize their input are prone to LDAP injection. This technique is similar to the popular SQL injection attack used against databases.

To better understand LDAP injection, consider a web application that uses LDAP for authentication. Such applications usually provide a web page that lets a user enter his user name and password. In order to verify that username and password match, the application would then construct an LDAP search query that looks more or less like this:

`(&(uid=USER_INPUT_UID)(password=USER_INPUT_PWD))`

Let's assume that the application simply trusts the user input and doesn't perform any validation. Now if you enter the text `jdoe)(&)(` as the user name and any random text as password, the resulting search query filter would look like this:

`(&(uid=jdoe)(&))((password=randomstr))`

If the username `jdoe` is a valid user id in LDAP, then regardless of the entered password, this query will always evaluate to true. This LDAP injection would allow an attacker to bypass authentication and get into the application. The "LDAP Injection & Blind LDAP Injection" article available at `www.blackhat.com/presentations/ bh-europe-08/Alonso-Parada/Whitepaper/bh-eu-08-alonso-parada-WP.pdf` discusses various LDAP injection techniques in great detail.

Preventing LDAP injection, and any other injection techniques in general, begins with proper input validation. It is important to sanitize the entered data and properly encode it before it is used in search filters.

Spring LDAP Filters

In the previous section, you learned that LDAP search filters are very important for narrowing down the search and identifying entries. However, creating LDAP filters dynamically can be tedious, especially when trying to combine multiple filters. Making sure that all the braces are properly closed can be error-prone. It is also important to escape special characters properly.

Spring LDAP provides several filter classes that make it easy to create and encode LDAP filters. All these filters implement the Filter interface and are part of the org.springframework.ldap.filter package. Listing 6-1 shows the Filter API interface.

Listing 6-1.

```
package org.springframework.ldap.filter;

public interface Filter {
    String encode();
    StringBuffer encode(StringBuffer buf);
    boolean equals(Object o);
    int hashCode();
}
```

The first encode method in this interface returns a string representation of the filter. The second encode method accepts a StringBuffer as its parameter and returns the encoded version of the filter as a StringBuffer. For your regular development process, you use the first version of encode method that returns String.

The Filter interface hierarchy is shown in Figure 6-2. From the hierarchy, you can see that AbstractFilter implements the Filter interface and acts as the root class for all other filter implementations. The BinaryLogicalFilter is the abstract superclass for binary logical operations such as AND and OR. The CompareFilter is the abstract superclass for filters that compare values such as EqualsFilter and LessThanOrEqualsFilter.

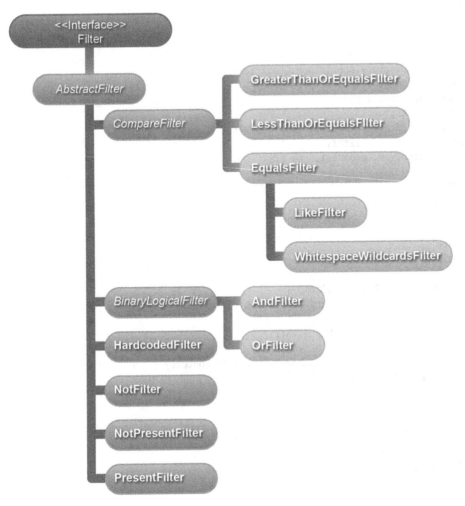

Figure 6-2. Filter hierarchy

■ **Note**   Most LDAP attribute values by default are case-insensitive for searches.

In the coming sections, you will look at each of the filters in Figure 6-2. Before you do that, let's create a reusable method that will help you test your filters. Listing 6-2 shows the searchAndPrintResults method that uses the passed-in Filter implementation parameter and performs a search using it. It then outputs the search results to the console. Notice that you will be searching the Patron branch of the LDAP tree.

Listing 6-2.

```
import java.util.List;
import org.springframework.beans.factory.annotation.Autowired;
import org.springframework.beans.factory.annotation.Qualifier;
import org.springframework.ldap.core.DirContextOperations;
import org.springframework.ldap.core.simple.
AbstractParameterizedContextMapper;
import org.springframework.ldap.core.simple.SimpleLdapTemplate;
import org.springframework.ldap.filter.Filter;
import org.springframework.stereotype.Component;

@Component("searchFilterDemo" )
public class SearchFilterDemo {

    @Autowired
    @Qualifier("ldapTemplate" )
    private SimpleLdapTemplate ldapTemplate;

    public void searchAndPrintResults(Filter filter) {
        List<String> results = ldapTemplate.search("ou=patrons,dc=inflinx,
        dc=com", filter.encode(),
                new AbstractParameterizedContextMapper<String>() {
                @Override
                protected String doMapFromContext(DirContextOperations context) {
                  return context.getStringAttribute("cn");
                }
            });

        System.out.println("Results found in search: " + results.size());
          for(String commonName: results) {
              System.out.println(commonName);
          }
      }
   }
}
```

EqualsFilter

An EqualsFilter can be used to retrieve all entries that have the specified attribute and value. Let's say you want to retrieve all patrons with the first name Jacob. To do this, you create a new instance of EqualsFilter.

```
EqualsFilter filter =  new  EqualsFilter("givenName", "Jacob");
```

The first parameter to the constructor is the attribute name and the second parameter is the attribute value. Invoking the encode method on this filter results in the string (givenName=Jacob).

Listing 6-3 shows the test case that invokes the searchAndPrintResults with the above EqualsFilter as parameter. The console output of the method is also shown in the Listing. Notice that the results have patrons with first name jacob (notice the lowercase j). That is because the sn attribute, like most LDAP attributes, is defined in the schema as being case-insensitive.

Listing 6-3.

```
@Test
public void testEqualsFilter() {
    Filter filter = new EqualsFilter("givenName", "Jacob");
    searchFilterDemo.searchAndPrintResults(filter);
}
```

```
Results  found in  search:  2
Jacob  Smith
jacob  Brady
```

LikeFilter

The LikeFilter is useful for searching LDAP when only a partial value of an attribute is known. The LDAP specification allows the usage of the wildcard * to describe these partial values. Say you want to retrieve all users whose first name begins with "Ja." To do this, you create a new instance of LikeFilter and pass in the wildcard substring as attribute value.

```
LikeFilter  filter =  new  LikeFilter("givenName", "Ja*");
```

Invoking the encode method on this filter results in the string (givenName=Ja*). Listing 6-4 shows the test case and the results of invoking the searchAndPrintResults method with the LikeFilter.

Listing 6-4.

```
@Test
public void testLikeFilter() {
    Filter filter = new LikeFilter("givenName", "Ja*");
    searchFilterDemo.searchAndPrintResults(filter);
}
```

```
Results  found in  search:  3
Jacob  Smith
Jason  Brown
jacob  Brady
```

The wildcard * in the substring is used to match zero or more characters. However, it is very important to understand that LDAP search filters do not support regular expressions. Table 6-2 lists some substring examples.

Table 6-2. *LDAP Substring Examples*

LDAP Substring	Description
(givenName=*son)	Matches all patrons whose first name ends with son.
(givenName=J*n)	Matches all patrons whose first name starts with J and ends with n.
(givenName=*a*)	Matches all patrons with first name containing the character a.
(givenName=J*s*n)	Matches patrons whose first name starts with J, contains character s, and ends with n.

You might be wondering about the necessity of a `LikeFilter` when you can accomplish the same filter expression by simply using the `EqualsFilter`, like this:

```
EqualsFilter filter =  new  EqualsFiler("uid", "Ja*");
```

Using `EqualsFilter` in this scenario will not work because the encode method in `EqualsFilter` considers the wildcard * in the `Ja*` as a special character and properly escapes it. Thus, the above filter when used for a search would result in all entries that have a first name starting with Ja*.

PresentFilter

`PresentFilters` are useful for retrieving LDAP entries that have at least one value in a given attribute. Consider the earlier scenario where you wanted to retrieve all the patrons that have an e-mail address. To do this, you create a `PresentFilter`, as shown:

```
PresentFilter presentFilter =  new  PresentFilter("email");
```

Invoking the encode method on the `presentFilter` instance results in the string (email=*). Listing 6-5 shows the test code and the result when the `searchAndPrintResults` method is invoked with the above `presentFilter`.

Listing 6-5.

```
@Test
public void testPresentFilter() {
    Filter filter = new PresentFilter("mail");
    searchFilterDemo.searchAndPrintResults(filter);
}

Results  found  in  search:  97
Jacob  Smith
Aaren  Atp
```

```
Aarika  Atpco
Aaron  Atrc
Aartjan  Aalders
Abagael  Aasen
Abagail  Abadines
.........
.........
```

NotPresentFilter

NotPresentFilters are used to retrieve entries that don't have a specified attribute. Attributes that do not have any value in an entry are considered to be not present. Now, let's say you want to retrieve all patrons that don't have an e-mail address. To do this, you create an instance of NotPresentFilter, as shown:

```
NotPresentFilter notPresentFilter  =  new NotPresentFilter("email");
```

The encoded version of the notPresentFilter results in the expression !(email=*). Running the searchAndPrintResults results in the output shown in Listing 6-6. The first null is for the organizational unit entry "ou=patrons,dc=inflinx,dc=com".

Listing 6-6.

```
@Test
public void testNotPresentFilter() {
    Filter filter = new NotPresentFilter("mail");
    searchFilterDemo.searchAndPrintResults(filter);
}

Results  found  in  search:  5
null
Addons Achkar
Adeniyi Adamowicz
Adoree Aderhold
Adorne  Adey
```

Not Filter

A NotFilter is useful for retrieving entries that do not match a given condition. In the "LikeFilter" section, you looked at retrieving all entries that start with Ja. Now let's say you want to retrieve all entries that don't start with Ja. This is where a NotFilter comes into picture. Here is the code for accomplishing this requirement:

```
NotFilter notFilter  =  new  NotFilter(new LikeFilter("givenName", "Ja*"));
```

Encoding this filter results in the string !(givenName=Ja*). As you can see, the NotFilter simply adds the negation symbol (!) to the filter passed into its constructor. Invoking the searchAndShowResults method results in the output shown in Listing 6-7.

Listing 6-7.

```
@Test
public void testNotFilter() {
    NotFilter notFilter = new NotFilter(new LikeFilter("givenName", "Ja*"));
    searchFilterDemo.searchAndPrintResults(notFilter);
}
```

```
Results  found  in  search:  99
Aaren Atp  Aarika
Atpco Aaron Atrc
Aartjan  Aalders
Abagael  Aasen
Abagail  Abadines
.......................
```

It is also possible to combine NotFilter and PresentFilter to create expressions that are equivalent to NotPresentFilter. Here is a new implementation that gets all the entries that don't have an e-mail address:

```
NotFilter notFilter  =  new  NotFilter(new PresentFilter("email"));
```

GreaterThanOrEqualsFilter

The GreaterThanOrEqualsFilter is useful for matching all entries that are lexicographically equal to or higher than the given attribute value. For example, a search expression (givenName >= Jacob) can be used to retrieve all entries with given name alphabetically after Jacob, in addition to Jacob. Listing 6-8 shows this implementation along with the output results.

Listing 6-8.

```
@Test
public void testGreaterThanOrEqualsFilter() {
    Filter filter = new GreaterThanOrEqualsFilter("givenName", "Jacob");
    searchFilterDemo.searchAndPrintResults(filter);
}
```

```
Results  found  in  search:  3
Jacob Smith
jacob Brady
Jason Brown
```

HardcodedFilter

The HardcodedFilter is a convenience class that makes it easy to add static filter text while building search filters. Let's say you are writing an admin application that allows the administrator to enter a search expression in a text box. If you want to use this expression along with other filters for a search, you can use HardcodedFilter, as shown:

```
AndFilter filter = new AndFilter();
filter.add(new HardcodedFilter(searchExpression));
filter.add(new EqualsFilter("givenName", "smith"));
```

In this code, the searchExpression variable contains the user-entered search expression. HardcodedFilter also comes in very handy when the static portion of a search filter comes from a properties file or a configuration file. It is important to remember that this filter does not encode the passed-in text. So please use it with caution, especially when dealing with user input directly.

WhitespaceWildcardsFilter

The WhitespaceWildcardsFilter is another convenience class that makes creation of sub-string search filters easier. Like its superclass EqualsFilter, this class takes an attribute name and a value. However, as the name suggests, it converts all whitespaces in the attribute value to wildcards. Consider the following example:

```
WhitespaceWildcardsFilter filter = new WhitespaceWildcardsFilter("cn", "John Will");
```

This filter results in the following expression: (cn=*John*Will*). This filter can be useful while developing search and lookup applications.

Creating Custom Filters

Even though the filter classes provided by Spring LDAP are sufficient in most cases, there might be scenarios where the current set is inadequate. Thankfully, Spring LDAP has made it easy to create new filter classes. In this section, you will look at creating a custom approximate filter.

Approximate filters are used to retrieve entries with attribute values approximately equal to the specified value. Approximate expressions are created using the ~= operator. So a filter of (givenName ~= Adeli) will match entries with first name such as Adel or Adele. The approximate filter is useful in search applications when the actual spelling of the value is not known to the user at the time of the search. The implementation of the algorithm to find phonetically similar values varies from one LDAP server implementation to another.

Spring LDAP does not provide any out-of-the-box class to create an approximate filter. In Listing 6-12, you create an implementation of this filter. Notice that the ApproximateFilter class extends the AbstractFilter. The constructor is defined to accept the attribute type and the attribute value. In the encode method, you construct the filter expression by concatenating the attribute type, operator, and the value.

Listing 6-12.

```
import org.springframework.ldap.filter.AbstractFilter;

private class ApproximateFilter extends AbstractFilter {

    private static final String APPROXIMATE_SIGN = "~=";
    private String attribute;
    private String value;

    public ApproximateFilter(String attribute, String value) {
        this.attribute = attribute;
        this.value = value;
    }

    @Override
    public StringBuffer encode(StringBuffer buff) {
        buff.append('(');
        buff.append(attribute).append(APPROXIMATE_SIGN).append(value);
        buff.append(')');

            return buff;
    }
}
```

Listing 6-13 shows the test code for running the searchAndPrintResults method with ApproximateFilter class.

Listing 6-13.

```
@Test
public void testApproximateFilter() {
    ApproximateFilter approx = new ApproximateFilter("givenName", "Adeli");
    searchFilterDemo.searchAndPrintResults(approx);
}
```

Here is the output of running the test case:

```
Results found in search: 6
Adel Acker
Adela Acklin
Adele Acres
Adelia Actionteam
Adella Adamczyk
Adelle Adamkowski
```

Handling Special Characters

There will be times when you need to construct search filters with characters such as
(or a * that have special meanings in LDAP. To execute these filters successfully, it is
important to escape the special characters properly. Escaping is done using the
format \xx where xx denotes the hexadecimal representation of the character. Table 6-3
lists all of the special characters along with their escape values.

Table 6-3. *Special Characters and Escape Values*

Special Character	Escape Value
(	\28
)	\29
*	\2a
\	\5c
/	\2f

In addition to the above characters, if any of the following characters are used in a
DN, they also need to be properly escaped: comma (,), equals sign (=), plus sign (+),
less than (<), greater than (>), pound sign (#), and semi-colon (;).

Summary

In this chapter, you learned how to simplify LDAP searches using search filters. I started
the chapter with an overview of LDAP search concepts. Then you looked at different
search filters that you can use to retrieve data in a variety of ways. You also saw how
Spring LDAP makes it easy to create custom search filters.

In the next chapter, you will look at sorting and paging the results obtained from an
LDAP server.

CHAPTER 7

■ ■ ■

Sorting and Paging Results

In this chapter you will learn

- The basics of LDAP controls.

- Sorting LDAP results.

- Paging LDAP results.

LDAP Controls

LDAP controls provide a standardized way to modify the behavior of LDAP operations. A control can be viewed simply as a message that a client sends to an LDAP server (or vice versa). Controls that are sent as part of a client request can provide additional information to the server indicating how the operation should be interpreted and executed. For example, a delete subtree control can be specified on an LDAP delete operation. Upon receiving a delete request, the default behavior of an LDAP server is to just delete the entry. However, when a delete subtree control is appended to the delete request, the server automatically deletes the entry as well as all its subordinate entries. Such controls are referred to as request controls.

It is also possible for LDAP servers to send controls as part of their response message indicating how the operation was processed. For example, an LDAP server may return a password policy control during a bind operation indicating that the client's password has expired or will be expiring soon. Such controls sent by the server are referred to as response controls. It is possible to send any number of request or response controls along with an operation.

LDAP controls, both request and response, are made up of the following three components:

- An Object Identifier (OID) that uniquely identifies the control. These OIDs prevent conflicts between control names and are usually defined by the vendor that creates the control. This is a required component of a control.

- Indication whether the control is critical or non-critical for the operation. This is also a required component and can be either TRUE or FALSE.

- Optional information specific to the control. For example, the paged control used for paging search results needs the page size to determine the number of entries to return in a page.

The formal definition of an LDAP control as specified in RFC 2251 (www.ietf.org/rfc/rfc2251.txt) is shown in Figure 7-1. This LDAP specification, however, does not define any concrete controls. Control definitions are usually provided by LDAP vendors and their support varies vastly from one server to another.

```
Controls ::= SEQUENCE Of Control

Control ::= SEQUENCE
    {
            controlType          LDAPOID,
            criticality          BOOLEAN DEFAULT FALSE,
            controlValue         OCTED STRING OPTIONAL
    }
```

Figure 7-1. *LDAP control specification*

When an LDAP server receives a control as part of an operation, its behavior is dependent on the control and its associated information. The flow chart in Figure 7-2 shows the server behavior upon receiving a request control.

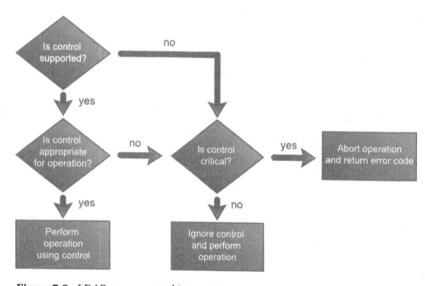

Figure 7-2. *LDAP server control interaction*

Some of the commonly supported LDAP controls along with their OID and description are shown in Table 7-1.

Table 7-1. *Commonly Used Controls*

Control Name	OID	Description (RFC)
Sort Control	1.2.840.113556.1.4.473	Requests the server to sort the search results before sending them to client. This is part of RFC 2891.
Paged Results Control	1.2.840.113556.1.4.319	Requests the server to return search results in pages consisting of specified number of entries. Only sequential iteration of the search results is allowed. This is defined as part of RFC 2696.
Subtree Delete Control	1.2.840.113556.1.4.805	Requests the server delete the entry and all its descendent entries.
Virtual List View Control	2.16.840.1.113730.3.4.9	This is similar to Page search results but allows client request arbitrary subsets of entries. This control is described in the Internet Drafts file VLV 04.
Password Policy Control	1.3.6.1.4.1.42.2.27.8.5.1	Server-sent control that holds information about failed operation (authentication, for example) due to password policy problems such as password needs to be reset or account has been locked or password has expired or expiring.
Manage DSA/IT Control	2.16.840.1.113730.3.4.2	Requests the server to treat "ref" attribute entries (referrals) as regular LDAP entries.
Persistent Search Control	2.16.840.1.113730.3.4.3	This control allows the client to receive notifications of changes in the LDAP server for entries that match a search criteria.

Identifying Supported Controls

Before a particular control can be used, it is important to make sure that the LDAP server you are using supports that control. The LDAP specification mandates every LDAP v3 compliant server publish all the supported controls in the supportedControl attribute of the Root *DSA-Specific Entry* (DSE). Thus, searching the Root DSE entry for the supportedControl attribute will list all the controls. Listing 7-1 shows the code that connects to the OpenDJ server running on port 11389 and prints the control list to the console.

Listing 7-1.

```java
package com.inflinx.book.ldap;

import java.util.Properties;
import javax.naming.NamingEnumeration;
import javax.naming.NamingException;
import javax.naming.directory.Attribute;
import javax.naming.directory.Attributes;
import javax.naming.directory.DirContext;
import javax.naming.directory.InitialDirContext;

public class SupportedControlApplication {

    public void displayControls() {

        String ldapUrl = "ldap://localhost:11389";
        try {
            Properties environment = new Properties();
            environment.setProperty(DirContext.INITIAL_CONTEXT_FACTORY,
            "com.sun.jndi.ldap.LdapCtxFactory");
            environment.setProperty(DirContext.PROVIDER_URL,ldapUrl);
            DirContext context = new InitialDirContext(environment);
            Attributes attributes = context.getAttributes("", new String[]
            {"supportedcontrol"});
            Attribute supportedControlAttribute = attributes.get("supportedcontrol");
            NamingEnumeration controlOIDList = supportedControlAttribute.getAll();
            while(controlOIDList != null && controlOIDList.hasMore()) {
                System.out.println(controlOIDList.next());
            }
            context.close();
        }
        catch(NamingException e) {
            e.printStackTrace();
        }
    }

    public static void main(String[] args) throws NamingException {
        SupportedControlApplication supportedControlApplication = new
        SupportedControlApplication();
        supportedControlApplication.displayControls();
    }
}
```

Here is the output after running the code from Listing 7-1:

```
1.2.826.0.1.3344810.2.3
1.2.840.113556.1.4.1413
1.2.840.113556.1.4.319
1.2.840.113556.1.4.473
1.2.840.113556.1.4.805
1.3.6.1.1.12
1.3.6.1.1.13.1
1.3.6.1.1.13.2
1.3.6.1.4.1.26027.1.5.2
1.3.6.1.4.1.42.2.27.8.5.1
1.3.6.1.4.1.42.2.27.9.5.2
1.3.6.1.4.1.42.2.27.9.5.8
1.3.6.1.4.1.4203.1.10.1
1.3.6.1.4.1.4203.1.10.2
2.16.840.1.113730.3.4.12
2.16.840.1.113730.3.4.16
2.16.840.1.113730.3.4.17
2.16.840.1.113730.3.4.18
2.16.840.1.113730.3.4.19
2.16.840.1.113730.3.4.2
2.16.840.1.113730.3.4.3
2.16.840.1.113730.3.4.4
2.16.840.1.113730.3.4.5
2.16.840.1.113730.3.4.9
```

The OpenDJ installation provides a command line ldapsearch tool that can also be used for listing the supported controls. Assuming that OpenDJ is installed under c:\practicalldap\opendj on Windows, here is the command to get a list of supported controls:

```
ldapsearch --baseDN "" --searchScope base --port 11389 "(objectclass=*)"
supportedControl
```

Figure 7-3 displays the results of running this command. Notice that in order to search Root DSE, you used the scope base and did not provide a base DN. Also, the supported control OIDs in the figure match the OIDs received after running the Java code in Listing 7-1.

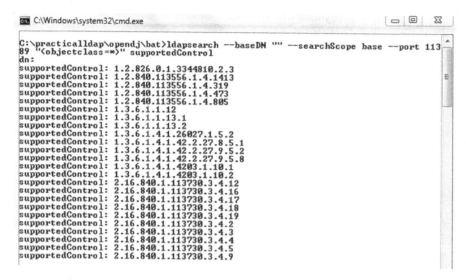

Figure 7-3. OpenDJ ldapsearch command

JNDI and Controls

The javax.naming.ldap package in the JNDI API contains support for LDAP V3-specific features such as controls and extended operations. While controls modify or augment the behavior of existing operations, extended operations allow additional operations to be defined. The UML diagram in Figure 7-4 highlights some of the important control classes in the javax.naming.ldap package.

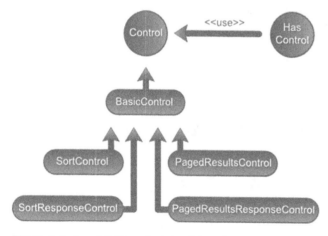

Figure 7-4. Java LDAP control class hierarchy

The javax.naming.ldap.Control interface provides abstraction for both request and response controls. Several implementations of this interface, such as SortControl and PagedResultsControl, are provided as part of the JDK. Additional controls, such as Virtual- ListViewControl and PasswordExpiringResponseControl, are available as part of the LDAP booster pack.

A core component in the javax.naming.ldap package is the LdapContext interface. This interface extends the javax.naming.DirContext interface and provides additional methods for performing LDAP V3 operations. The InitialLdapContext class in the javax.naming.ldap package provides a concrete implementation of this interface.

Using controls with JNDI API is a very straightforward. The code in Listing 7-2 provides the algorithm for using controls.

Listing 7-2.

```
LdapContext context = new InitialLdapContext();
Control[] requestControls = // Concrete control instance array
context.setRequestControls(requestControls);
/* Execute a search operation using the context*/
context.search(parameters);
Control[] responseControls = context.getResponseControls();
// Analyze the response controls
```

In this algorithm, you start by creating instances of the controls that you would like to include in the request operation. Then you perform the operation and process the results of the operation. Finally, you analyze any response controls that the server has sent over. In the coming sections, you will look at concrete implementations of this algorithm in conjunction with sort and paging controls.

Spring LDAP and Controls

Spring LDAP does not provide access to a directory context when working with LdapTemplate's search methods. As a result, you don't have a way to add request controls to the context or process response controls. To address this, Spring LDAP provides a directory context processor that automates the addition and analysis of LDAP controls to a context. Listing 7-3 shows the DirContextProcessor API code.

Listing 7-3.

```
package org.springframework.ldap.core;

import javax.naming.NamingException;
import javax.naming.directory.DirContext;

public interface DirContextProcessor {
    void preProcess(DirContext ctx) throws NamingException;
    void postProcess(DirContext ctx) throws NamingException;
}
```

Concrete implementations of the DirContextProcessor interface are passed to the LdapTemplate's search methods. The preProcess method gets called before a search is performed. Hence, the concrete implementations will have logic in the preProcess method to add request controls to the context. The postProcess method will be called after the search execution. So, the concrete implementations will have logic in the postProcess method to read and analyze any response controls that the LDAP server would have sent.

Figure 7-5 shows the UML representation of the DirContextProcessor and all its implementations.

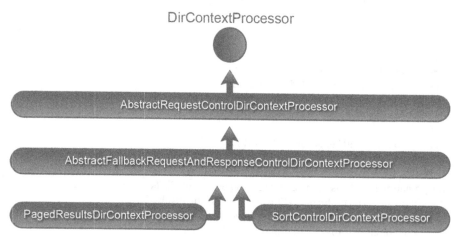

Figure 7-5. *DirContextProcessor class hierarchy*

The AbstractRequestControlDirContextProcessor implements the preProcess method of the DirContextProcessor and applies a single RequestControl on an LdapContext. The AbstractRequestDirContextProcessor delegates the actual creation of the request controls to the subclasses through the createRequestControl template method.

The AbstractFallbackRequestAndResponseControlDirContextProcessor class extends the AbstractRequestControlDirContextProcessor and makes heavy use of reflection to automate DirContext processing. It performs the tasks of loading control classes, creating their instances, and applying them to the context. It also takes care of most of the post processing of the response control, delegating a template method to the subclass that does the actual value retrieval.

The PagedResultsDirContextProcessor and SortControlDirContextProcessor are used for managing paging and sorting controls. You will be looking at them in the coming sections.

Sort Control

The sort control provides a mechanism to request an LDAP server sort the results of a search operation before sending them over to the client. This control is specified in RFC 2891 (`www.ietf.org/rfc/rfc2891.txt`). The sort request control accepts one or more LDAP attribute names and supplies it to the server to perform the actual sorting.

Let's look at using the sort control with plain JNDI API. Listing 7-4 shows the code for sorting all search results by their last names. You start by creating a new instance of the `javax.naming.ldap.SortControl` and provide it with the sn attribute indicating your intention to sort by last name. You have also indicated that this is a critical control by providing the CRITICAL flag to the same constructor. This request control is then added to the context using the `setRequestControls` method and the LDAP search operation is performed. You then loop through the returned results and print them to the console. Finally, you look at the response controls. The sort response control holds the result of the sort operation. If the server failed to sort the results, you indicate this by throwing an exception.

Listing 7-4.

```
public void sortByLastName() {
    try {
        LdapContext context = getContext();
        Control lastNameSort = new SortControl("sn", Control.CRITICAL);
        context.setRequestControls(new Control[]{lastNameSort});
        SearchControls searchControls = new SearchControls();
        searchControls.setSearchScope( SearchControls.SUBTREE_SCOPE);
        NamingEnumeration results = context.search("dc=inflinx,dc=com",
        "(objectClass=inetOrgPerson)", searchControls);

            /* Iterate over search results and display
      * patron entries
      */
        while (results != null && results.hasMore()) {
            SearchResult entry = (SearchResult)results.next();
            System.out.println(entry.getAttributes().get("sn") +
            " ( " + (entry.getName()) + " )");
        }

        /* Now that we have looped, we need to look at the response controls*/
        Control[] responseControls = context.getResponseControls();
        if(null != responseControls) {
            for(Control control : responseControls) {
                if(control instanceof SortResponseControl) {
                    SortResponseControl sortResponseControl =
                    (SortResponseControl) control;
```

```
                    if(!sortResponseControl.isSorted()) {
                        // Sort did not happen. Indicate this with an exception
                        throw sortResponseControl.getException();
                    }
                }
            }
        }
    }
    context.close();
}
catch(Exception e) {
    e.printStackTrace();
}
}
```

The output should display the sorted patrons as shown below:
```
sn: Aalders ( uid=patron4,ou=patrons )
sn: Aasen ( uid=patron5,ou=patrons )
sn: Abadines ( uid=patron6,ou=patrons )
sn: Abazari ( uid=patron7,ou=patrons )
sn: Abbatantuono ( uid=patron8,ou=patrons )
sn: Abbate ( uid=patron9,ou=patrons )
sn: Abbie ( uid=patron10,ou=patrons )
sn: Abbott ( uid=patron11,ou=patrons )
sn: Abdalla ( uid=patron12,ou=patrons )
. . . . . . . . . . . . . . . . . . . . . . . . . . . . . . . . . . .
```

Now let's look at implementing the same sort behavior using Spring LDAP. Listing 7-5 shows the associated code. In this implementation, you start out by creating a new org.springframework.ldap.control.SortControlDirContextProcessor instance. The SortControlDirContextProcessor constructor takes the LDAP attribute name that should be used as the sort key during control creation. The next step is to create the SearchControls and a filter to limit the search. Finally, you invoke the search method, passing in the created instances along with a mapper to map the data.

Listing 7-5.
```
public List<String> sortByLastName() {
    DirContextProcessor scdcp = new SortControlDirContextProcessor("sn");
    SearchControls searchControls = new SearchControls();
    searchControls.setSearchScope(SearchControls.SUBTREE_SCOPE);

    EqualsFilter equalsFilter = new EqualsFilter("objectClass",
    "inetOrgPerson");

    @SuppressWarnings("unchecked")
    ParameterizedContextMapper<String> lastNameMapper = new AbstractParameter
    izedContextMapper<String>() {
```

```
    @Override
    protected String doMapFromContext(DirContextOperations context) {
        return context.getStringAttribute("sn");
    }
};

List<String> lastNames = ldapTemplate.search("", equalsFilter.encode(),
searchControls, lastNameMapper, scdcp);
for (String ln : lastNames){
    System. out .println(ln);
}
return lastNames;
}
```

Upon invoking this method, you should see the following output in the console:

```
Aalders
Aasen
Abadines
Abazari
Abbatantuono
Abbate
Abbie
Abbott
Abdalla
Abdo
Abdollahi
Abdou
Abdul-Nour
. . . . . . . . . . . . . . . .
```

Implementing Custom DirContextProcessor

As of Spring LDAP 1.3.2, SortControlDirContextProcessor can be used to sort only on one LDAP attribute. The JNDI API, however, allows you to sort on multiple attributes. Since there will be cases where you would like to sort your search results on multiple attributes, let's implement a new DirContextProcessor that will allow you to do this in Spring LDAP.

As you have seen so far, the sort operation requires a request control and will send a response control. So the easiest way to implement this functionality is to extend the AbstractFallbackRequestAndResponseControlDirContextProcessor. Listing 7-6 shows the initial code with empty abstract methods implementation. As you will see, you are using three instance variables to hold the state of the control. The sortKeys, as the name suggests, will hold the attribute names that you will be sorting on. The sorted and the resultCode variables will hold the information extracted from the response control.

Listing 7-6.

```
package com.inflinx.book.ldap.control;

import javax.naming.ldap.Control;
import org.springframework.ldap.control.
AbstractFallbackRequestAndResponseControlDirContextProcessor;

public class SortMultipleControlDirContextProcessor extends
AbstractFallbackRequestAndResponseControlDirContextProcessor {

    //The keys to sort on
    private String[] sortKeys;

    //Did the results actually get sorted?
    private boolean sorted;

    //The result code of the sort operation
    private int resultCode;

    @Override
    public Control createRequestControl() {
        return null;
    }

    @Override
    protected void handleResponse(Object control) {
    }

    public String[] getSortKeys() {
        return sortKeys;
    }

    public boolean isSorted() {
        return sorted;
    }

    public int getResultCode() {
        return resultCode;
    }
}
```

The next step is to provide necessary information to
AbstractFallbackRequestAndResponseControlDirContextProcessor for loading the
controls. The AbstractFallbackRequestAndResponseControlDirContextProcessor
expects two pieces of information from subclasses: the fully qualified class names of the
request and response controls to be used, and the fully qualified class names of the controls
that should be used as fallback. Listing 7-7 shows the constructor code that does this.

Listing 7-7.

```
public SortMultipleControlDirContextProcessor(String ... sortKeys) {

    if(sortKeys.length == 0) {
        throw new IllegalArgumentException("You must provide " + "atlease one
        key to sort on");
    }

    this.sortKeys = sortKeys;
    this.sorted = false;
    this.resultCode = -1;
    this.defaultRequestControl = "javax.naming.ldap.SortControl";
    this.defaultResponseControl = "javax.naming.ldap.SortResponseControl";
    this.fallbackRequestControl = "com.sun.jndi.ldap.ctl.SortControl";
    this.fallbackResponseControl = "com.sun.jndi.ldap.ctl.SortResponseControl";

    loadControlClasses();
}
```

Notice that you have provided the control classes that come with the JDK as the
default controls to be used and the controls that come with the LDAP booster pack
as the fallback controls. On the last line of the constructor, you instruct the
AbstractFallbackRequestAndResponseControlDirContextProcessor class to load the
classes into JVM for usage.

The next step in the process is to provide implementation to the
createRequestControl method. Since the superclass
AbstractFallbackRequestAndResponseControlDirContextProcessor will take care
of the actual creation of the control, all you need to do is to provide the information
necessary for creating the control. The following code shows this:

```
@Override
public Control createRequestControl() {
    return super.createRequestControl(new Class[] {String[].class,
    boolean.class }, new Object[] { sortKeys, critical });
}
```

The final step in the implementation is to analyze the response control and retrieve
the information regarding the completed operation. Listing 7-8 shows the code involved.
Notice that you are using reflection to retrieve the sorted and result code information
from the response control.

Listing 7-8.

```
@Override
protected void handleResponse(Object control) {

    Boolean result = (Boolean) invokeMethod("isSorted", responseControlClass,
    control);
    this.sorted = result;

    Integer code = (Integer) invokeMethod("getResultCode",
    responseControlClass, control);
    this.resultCode = code;
}
```

Now that you have created a new DirContextProcessor instance that allows you to sort on multiple attributes, let's take it for a spin. Listing 7-9 shows a sort method that uses the SortMultipleControlDirContextProcessor. The method uses the attributes st and l for sorting the results.

Listing 7-9.

```
public void sortByLocation() {

    String[] locationAttributes = {"st", "l"};
    SortMultipleControlDirContextProcessor smcdcp = new SortMultipleControlDir
    ContextProcessor(locationAttributes);
    SearchControls searchControls = new SearchControls();
    searchControls.setSearchScope(SearchControls.SUBTREE_SCOPE);

    EqualsFilter equalsFilter = new EqualsFilter("objectClass","inetOrgPerson");

    @SuppressWarnings("unchecked")
    ParameterizedContextMapper<String> locationMapper = new AbstractParameterized
    ContextMapper<String>() {

        @Override
        protected String doMapFromContext(DirContextOperations context) {
            return context.getStringAttribute("st") + "," + context.
            getStringAttribute("l");
        }
    };
```

```
List<String> results = ldapTemplate.search("", equalsFilter.encode(),
searchControls, locationMapper, smcdcp);
for(String r : results) {
    System.out.println(r);
}
}
```

Upon invoking the method, the sorted locations will be displayed on the console as shown:

```
AK,Abilene
AK,Florence
AK,Sioux Falls
AK,Wilmington
AL,Glendive
AR,Gainesville
AR,Green Bay
AZ,Gainesville
AZ,Moline
AZ,Reno
AZ,Saint Joseph
AZ,Wilmington
CA,Buffalo
CA,Ottumwa
CO,Charlottesville
CO,Lake Charles
CT,Quincy
CT,Youngstown
. . . . . . . . . . . . . . . .
```

Paged Search Controls

The paged results control allows LDAP clients to control the rate at which the results of an LDAP search operation are returned. The LDAP clients create a page control with a specified page size and associate it with the search request. Upon receiving the request, the LDAP server will return the results in chunks, with each chunk containing the specified number of results. The paged results control is highly useful when dealing with large directories or building search applications with paging capabilities. This control is described in RFC 2696 (www.ietf.org/rfc/rfc2696.txt).

Figure 7-6 describes the interaction between the LDAP client and server using a page control.

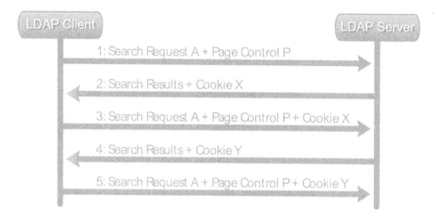

Figure 7-6. *Page control interaction*

■ **Note** LDAP servers often use the `sizeLimit` directive to restrict the number of results that are returned for a search operation. If a search produces more results than the specified `sizeLimit`, a size limit exceeded exception `javax.naming.SizeLimitExceededException` is thrown. The `paging` method does not let you pass through this limit.

As a first step, the LDAP client sends the search request along with the page control. Upon receiving the request, the LDAP server executes the search operation and returns the first page of results. Additionally, it sends a cookie that needs to be used to request the next paged results set. This cookie enables the LDAP server to maintain the search state. The client must not make any assumptions about the internal structure of the cookie. When the client makes a request for the next batch of results, it sends the same search request and page control, and the cookie. The server responds with the new result set and a new cookie. When there are no more search results to be returned, the server sends an empty cookie.

Paging using the paged search control is unidirectional and sequential. It is not possible for the client to jump between pages or go back. Now that you know the basics of the paging control, Listing 7-10 shows its implementation using the plain JNDI API.

Listing 7-10.

```java
public void pageAll() {

    try {
        LdapContext context = getContext();
        PagedResultsControl prc = new PagedResultsControl(20, Control.CRITICAL);
        context.setRequestControls(new Control[]{prc});
        byte[] cookie = null;
```

```java
SearchControls searchControls = new SearchControls();
searchControls.setSearchScope(SearchControls.SUBTREE_SCOPE);
do {
    NamingEnumeration results = context.search("dc=inflinx,dc=com",
    "(objectClass=inetOrgPerson)",searchControls);
    // Iterate over search results
    while(results != null && results.hasMore()) {
      // Display an entry
      SearchResult entry = (SearchResult)results.next();
      System.out.println(entry.getAttributes().get("sn") +
      " ( " + (entry.getName())+ " )");
    }
    // Examine the paged results control response
    Control[] controls = context.getResponseControls();
    if (controls != null) {
      for(int i = 0; i < controls.length; i++) {
        if(controls[i] instanceof PagedResultsResponseControl) {
          PagedResultsResponseControl prrc =(PagedResultsResponseControl)
          controls[i];
          int resultCount = prrc.getResultSize();
          cookie = prrc.getCookie();
        }
      }
    }
    // Re-activate paged results
    context.setRequestControls(new Control[]{
    new PagedResultsControl(20, cookie, Control.CRITICAL)});
} while(cookie != null);

    context.close();
  }
  catch(Exception e) {
    e.printStackTrace();
  }
}
```

In Listing 7-10, you start the implementation by obtaining a context on the LDAP server. Then you create the PagedResultsControl and specify the page size as its constructor parameter. You add the control to the context and performed the search operation. Then you loop through the search results and display the information on the console. As the next step, you examine the response controls to indentify the server sent PagedResultsResponseControl. From that control you extract the cookie and an estimated total number of results for this search. The result count is optional information and the server can simply return zero indicating that unknown count. Finally, you create a new PagedResultsControl with the page size and the cookie as its constructor parameter. This process is repeated until the server sends an empty (null) cookie indicating that there are no more results to be processed.

Spring LDAP abstracts most of the code in Listing 7-10 and makes it easy to deal with page controls using the PagedResultsDirContextProcessor. Listing 7-11 shows the Spring LDAP code.

Listing 7-11.

```
public void pagedResults() {

    PagedResultsCookie cookie = null;
    SearchControls searchControls = new SearchControls();
    searchControls.setSearchScope(SearchControls.SUBTREE_SCOPE);
    int page = 1;
    do {
        System.out.println("Starting Page: " + page);
        PagedResultsDirContextProcessor processor = new PagedResultsDirContext
        Processor(20,cookie);
        EqualsFilter equalsFilter = new EqualsFilter("objectClass","inetOrgPerson");
        List<String> lastNames = ldapTemplate.search("", equalsFilter.encode(),
        searchControls, new LastNameMapper(), processor);
        for(String l : lastNames) {
            System.out.println(l);
        }
        cookie = processor.getCookie();
        page = page + 1;
    } while(null != cookie.getCookie());
}
```

In this implementation, you create the PagedResultsDirContextProcessor with the page size and a cookie. Note that you are using the org.springframework.ldap.control.PagedResultsCookie class for abstracting the cookie sent by the server. The cookie value initially starts with a null. Then you perform the search and loop through the results. The cookie sent by the server is extracted from the DirContextProcessor and is used to check for future search requests. You are also using a LastNameMapper class to extract the last name from the results context. Listing 7-12 gives the implementation of the LastNameMapper class.

Listing 7-12.

```
private class LastNameMapper extends AbstractParameterizedContextMapper<String> {

    @Override
    protected String doMapFromContext(DirContextOperations context) {
        return context.getStringAttribute("sn");
    }
}
```

Summary

In this chapter you learned the basic concepts associated with LDAP controls. You then looked at the sort control, which can be used to perform server-side sorting of the results. You saw how Spring LDAP simplifies the sort control usage significantly. The paging control can be used to page LDAP results, which can be very useful under heavy traffic conditions.

In the next chapter, you will look at using Spring LDAP ODM technology for implementing the data access layer.

CHAPTER 8

■ ■ ■

Object-Directory Mapping

In this chapter, you will learn

- The basics of ODM.

- Spring LDAP ODM implementation.

Enterprise Java developers employ object-oriented (OO) techniques to create modular, complex applications. In the OO paradigm, objects are central to the system and represent entities in the real world. Each object has an identity, state, and behavior. Objects can be related to other objects through inheritance or composition. LDAP directories, on the other hand, represent data and relationships in a hierarchical tree structure. This difference leads to an object-directory paradigm mismatch and can cause problems in communication between OO and directory environments.

Spring LDAP provides an Object-Directory Mapping (ODM) framework that bridges the gap between the object and directory models. The ODM framework allows us to map concepts between the two models and orchestrates the process of automatically transforming LDAP directory entries into Java objects. ODM is similar to the more familiar Object-Relational Mapping (ORM) methodology that bridges the gap between object and relational database worlds. Frameworks such as Hibernate and Toplink have made ORM popular and an important part of the developer's toolset.

Though Spring LDAP ODM shares the same concepts as ORM, it does have the following differences:

- Caching of LDAP entries is not possible.

- ODM metadata is expressed through class-level annotations.

- No XML configuration is available.

- Lazy loading of entries is not possible.

- A query language, such as HQL, does not exist. Loading of objects is done via DN lookups and standard LDAP search queries.

Spring ODM Basics

The Spring LDAP ODM is distributed as a separate module from the core LDAP project. To include the Spring LDAP ODM in the project, the following dependency needs to be added to project's pom.xml file:

```
<dependency>
    <groupId>org.springframework.ldap</groupId>
    <artifactId>spring-ldap-odm</artifactId>
    <version>${org.springframework.ldap.version}</version>
    <exclusions>
        <exclusion>
            <artifactId>commons-logging</artifactId>
            <groupId>commons-logging</groupId>
        </exclusion>
    </exclusions>
</dependency>
```

The Spring LDAP ODM is available under the org.springframework.ldap.odm package and its subpackages. The core classes of Spring LDAP ODM are represented in Figure 8-1. You will look at each of these classes in detail throughout this chapter.

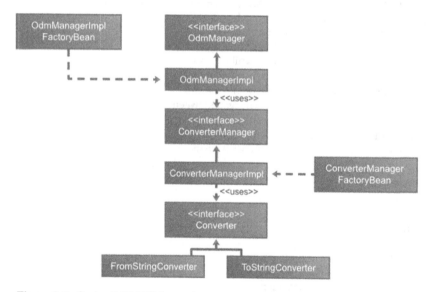

Figure 8-1. *Spring LAP ODM core classes*

Central to the LDAP ODM is the OdmManager that provides generic search and CRUD operations. It acts as a mediator and transforms data between LDAP entries and Java objects. The Java objects are annotated to provide the transformation metadata. Listing 8-1 shows the OdmManager API.

Listing 8-1.

```
Package org.springframworkldap.odm.core;

import java.util.List;
import javax.naming.Name;
import javax.naming.directory.SearchControls;

public interface OdmManager {

    void create(Object entry);
    <T> T read(Class<T> clazz, Name dn);
    void update(Object entry);
    void delete(Object entry);
    <T> List<T> findAll(Class<T> clazz, Name base, SearchControls
    searchControls);
    <T> List<T> search(Class<T> clazz, Name base, String filter,
    SearchControls searchControls);
}
```

The OdmManager's create, update, and delete methods take a Java object and use the information in it to perform corresponding LDAP operations. The read method takes two parameters, a Java class that determines the type to return and a fully qualified DN that is used to look up the LDAP entry. The OdmManager can be viewed as a slight variation on the Generic DAO pattern you saw in Chapter 5.

Spring LDAP ODM provides an out-of-the-box implementation of the OdmManager, the aptly named OdmManagerImpl. In order to function properly, an OdmManagerImpl uses the following three objects:

- A ContextSource implementation for communicating with the LDAP Server.

- A ConverterManager implementation to convert LDAP data types to Java data types and vice versa.

- A set of domain classes that needs to be managed by the ODM implementation.

To simplify the creation of OdmManagerImpl instances, the framework provides a factory bean, OdmManagerImplFactoryBean. Here is the necessary configuration for creating OdmManager instances:

```
<bean  id="odmManager" class="org.springframework.ldap.odm. core.impl.
OdmManagerImplFactoryBean">
    <property  name="converterManager" ref="converterManager"  />
    <property  name="contextSource" ref="contextSource" />
    <property  name="managedClasses">
```

```
        <set>
            <value>FULLY_QUALIFIED_CLASS_NAME</value>
        </set>
    </property>
</bean>
```

The `OdmManager` delegates the conversion management of the LDAP attributes to Java fields (and vice versa) to a `ConverterManager`. The `ConverterManager` itself relies on a set of `Converter` instances for the actual conversion purposes. Listing 8-2 shows the `Converter` interface API. The convert method accepts an object as its first parameter and converts it into an instance of the type specified by the `toClass` parameter.

Listing 8-2.

```
package org.springframework.ldap.odm.typeconversion.impl;

public interface Converter {
    <T> T convert(Object source, Class<T> toClass) throws Exception;
}
```

The generic nature of the converters makes it easy to create specific implementations. Spring LDAP ODM provides a `ToStringConverter` implementation of the `Converter` interface that converts the given source object into a String. Listing 8-3 provides the `ToStringConverter` API implementation. As you can see, the conversion takes place by simply invoking the `toString` method on the source object.

Listing 8-3.

```
package org.springframework.ldap.odm.typeconversion.impl.converters;

import org.springframework.ldap.odm.typeconversion.impl.Converter;

public final class ToStringConverter implements Converter {

    public <T> T convert(Object source, Class<T> toClass) {
        return toClass.cast(source.toString());
    }
}
```

The inverse of this implementation is the `FromStringConverter`, which converts a `java.lang.String` object into any specified `toClass` type. Listing 8-4 provides the `FromStringConverter` API implementation. The converter implementation creates a new instance by invoking the `toClass` parameter's constructor and passing in the String object. The `toClass` type parameter must have a public constructor that accepts a single `java.lang.String` type parameter. For example, the `FromStringConverter` can convert String data to an Integer or Long data type.

Listing 8-4.

```
package org.springframework.ldap.odm.typeconversion.impl.converters;

import java.lang.reflect.Constructor;
import org.springframework.ldap.odm.typeconversion.impl.Converter;

public final class FromStringConverter implements Converter {

    public <T> T convert(Object source, Class<T> toClass) throws Exception {
        Constructor<T> constructor = toClass.getConstructor(java.lang.String.class);
        return constructor.newInstance(source);
    }
}
```

These two converter classes should be sufficient for converting most LDAP data types to common Java field types such as `java.lang.Integer`, `java.lang.Byte`, etc. and vice versa. Listing 8-5 shows the XML configuration involved in creating `FromStringConverter` and `ToStringConverter` instances.

Listing 8-5.

```
<bean id="fromStringConverter" class="org.springframework.ldap.odm.
typeconversion.impl.converters.FromStringConverter" />
<bean id="toStringConverter" class="org.springframework.ldap.odm.
typeconversion.impl.converters.ToStringConverter" />
```

Now you are ready to create an instance of `ConverterManager` and register the above two converters with it. Registering a converter involves specifying the converter itself, a `fromClass` indicating the type of the source object the converter is expecting, and a `toClass` indicating the type the converter will return. To simplify the Converter registration process, Spring ODM provides a `ConverterConfig` class. Listing 8-6 shows the XML configuration for registering the `toStringConverter` instance.

Listing 8-6.

```
<bean id="toStringConverter" class="org.springframework.ldap.odm.
typeconversion.impl.ConverterManagerFactoryBean$ConverterConfig">
    <property name="converter" ref="toStringConverter"/>
    <property name="fromClasses">
        <set>
            <value>java.lang.Integer</value>
        </set>
    </property>
```

```
<property name="toClasses">
    <set>
        <value>java.lang.String</value>
    </set>
</property>
</bean>
```

As you can see, ConverterConfig is an inner class of the org.springframework.
ldap.odm.typeconversion.impl.ConverterManagerFactoryBean class. This
configuration tells the ConverterManager to use the toStringConverter bean for
converting java.lang.Integer types to String types. Internally, the converter is
registered under a key that is computed using the following algorithm:

```
key = fromClass.getName() + ":" + syntax + ":" + toClass. getName();
```

Sometimes you would like the same converter instance to be used for converting
from a variety of data types. The ToStringConverter, for example, can be used to convert
additional types such as java.lang.Long, java.lang.Byte, java.lang.Boolean, etc.
To address such scenarios, the ConverterConfig accepts a set of from and to classes that
the converter can deal with. Listing 8-7 shows the modified ConverterConfig that accepts
several fromClasses.

Listing 8-7.

```
<bean id="toStringConverter" class="org.springframework.ldap.odm.
typeconversion.impl.ConverterManagerFactoryBean$ConverterConfig">
    <property name="converter" ref="toStringConverter" />
    <property name="fromClasses">
        <set>
            <value>java.lang.Byte</value>
            <value>java.lang.Integer</value>
            <value>java.lang.Boolean</value>
        </set>
    </property>
    <property name="toClasses">
        <set>
            <value>java.lang.String</value>
        </set>
    </property>
</bean>
```

Each class specified in the above fromClasses set would be paired with a class
in the toClasses set for converter registration. So if you specify n fromClasses and
m toClasses, it would result in n*m registrations for the converter. Listing 8-8 shows
fromStringConverterConfig, which is quite similar to the previous configuration.

Listing 8-8.

```xml
<bean id="fromStringConverterConfig" class="org.springframework.ldap.odm.
typeconversion.impl.ConverterManagerFactoryBean$ConverterConfig">
   <property name="converter" ref="fromStringConverter" />
   <property name="fromClasses">
      <set>
         <value>java.lang.String</value>
      </set>
   </property>
   <property name="toClasses">
      <set>
         <value>java.lang.Byte</value>
         <value>java.lang.Integer</value>
         <value>java.lang.Boolean</value>
      </set>
   </property>
</bean>
```

Once you have the necessary converter configuration, new `ConverterManager` instances can be created using the `ConverterManagerFactoryBean`. Listing 8-9 shows the required XML declaration.

Listing 8-9.

```xml
<bean id="converterManager" class="org.springframework.ldap.odm.
typeconversion.impl.ConverterManagerFactoryBean">
   <property name="converterConfig">
      <set>
         <ref bean="fromStringConverterConfig"/>
         <ref bean="toStringConverterConfig"/>
      </set>
   </property>
</bean>
```

This concludes the setup needed for using the ODM framework. In the next sections, you will look at annotating the domain classes and using this configuration for LDAP reads and writes. Before you do that, let's recap what you did up to this point (see Figure 8-2).

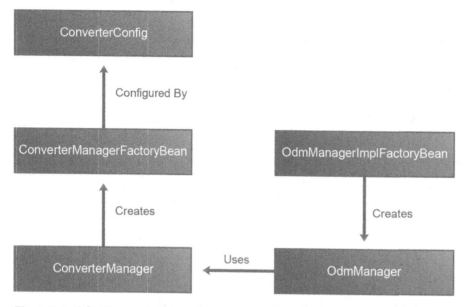

Figure 8-2. OdmManager inner workings

1. OdmManager instances are created by OdmManagerImplFactoryBean.

2. OdmManager uses ConverterManager instances for conversion between LDAP and Java types.

3. For the conversion from a specific type to another specific type, the ConverterManager uses a converter.

4. ConverterManager instances are created by ConverterManagerFactoryBean.

5. The ConverterManagerFactoryBean uses the ConverterConfig instances to simplify the Converter registration. The ConverterConfig class takes the fromClasses, toClasses, and the converter that goes along with the relationship.

ODM Metadata

The org.springframework.ldap.odm.annotations package contains annotations that can be used to turn simple Java POJOs into ODM manageable entities. Listing 8-10 shows the Patron Java class that you will convert into an ODM entity.

Listing 8-10.

```
public class Patron {

    private String lastName;
    private String firstName;
    private String telephoneNumber;
    private String fullName;
    private String mail;
    private int employeeNumber;

    // Getters and setters

    @Override
    public String toString() {
        return "Dn: " + dn + ", firstName: " + firstName + ", fullName: " +
        fullName + ", Telephone Number: " + telephoneNumber;
    }
}
```

You will start the conversion by annotating the class with @Entry. This marker annotation tells the ODM Manager that the class is an entity. It is also used to provide the objectClass definitions in LDAP that the entity maps to. Listing 8-11 shows the annotated Patron class.

Listing 8-11.

```
@Entry(objectClasses = { "inetorgperson", "organizationalperson", "person", "top" })
public class Patron {
    // Fields and getters and setters
}
```

The next annotation you need to add is the @Id. This annotation specifies the entry's DN and can only be placed on a field that is a derivative of javax.naming.Name class. To address this, you will create a new field called dn in the Patron class. Listing 8-12 shows the modified Patron class.

Listing 8-12.

```
@Entry(objectClasses = { "inetorgperson", "organizationalperson", "person", "top" })
public class Patron {

    @Id
    private Name dn;
    // Fields and getters and setters
}
```

The @Id annotation in the Java Persistence API specifies the identifier property of the entity bean. Additionally, its placement determines the default access strategy the JPA provider will use for mapping. If the @Id is placed over a field, field access is used. If it is placed over a getter method, property access will be used. However, Spring LDAP ODM only allows field access.

The @Entry and @Id are the only two required annotations to make the Patron class an ODM entity. By default, all the fields in the Patron entity class will automatically become persistable. The default strategy is to use the name of the entity field as the LDAP attribute name while persisting or reading. In the Patron class, this would work for attributes such as telephoneNumber or mail because the field name and the LDAP attribute name are the same. But this would cause problems with fields such as firstName and fullName as their names are different from the LDAP attribute names. To address this, ODM provides the @Attribute annotation that maps the entity fields to object class fields. This annotation allows you to specify the name of the LDAP attribute, an optional syntax OID, and an optional type declaration. Listing 8-13 shows the completely annotated Patron entity class.

Listing 8-13.

```
@Entry(objectClasses = { "inetorgperson", "organizationalperson", "person", "top" })
public class Patron {

    @Id
    private Name dn;

    @Attribute(name = "sn")
    private String lastName;

    @Attribute(name = "givenName")
    private String firstName;
    private String telephoneNumber;

    @Attribute(name = "cn")
    private String fullName;
    private String mail;

    @Attribute(name = "objectClass")
    private List<String> objectClasses;

    @Attribute(name = "employeeNumber", syntax = "2.16.840.1.113730.3.1.3")
    private int employeeNumber;

    // Getters and setters

    @Override
    public String toString() {
        return "Dn: " + dn + ", firstName: " + firstName + "," + " fullName: "
        + fullName + ", Telephone Number: " + telephoneNumber;
    }
}
```

There are times where you wouldn't want to persist certain fields of an entity class. Typically these involve fields that are computed. Such fields can be annotated with @Transient annotation indicating that the field should be ignored by OdmManager.

ODM Service Class

Spring-based enterprise applications typically have a service layer that holds the application's business logic. Classes in the service layer delegate persistent specifics to a DAO or Repository layer. In Chapter 5, you implemented a DAO using LdapTemplate. In this section, you will create a new service class that uses the OdmManager as a DAO replacement. Listing 8-14 shows the interface of the service class you will be implementing.

Listing 8-14.

```
package com.inflinx.book.ldap.service;

import com.inflinx.book.ldap.domain.Patron;

public interface PatronService {

    public void create(Patron patron);
    public void delete(String id);
    public void update(Patron patron);
    public Patron find(String id);
}
```

The service class implementation is given in Listing 8-15. In the implementation, you inject an instance of OdmManager. The create and update method implementations simply delegate the calls to the OdmManager. The find method converts the passed-in id parameter to the fully qualified DN and delegates the actual retrieval to OdmManager's read method. Finally, the delete method uses the find method to read the patron and uses the OdmManager's delete method to delete it.

Listing 8-15.

```
package com.inflinx.book.ldap.service;

import org.springframework.beans.factory.annotation.Autowired;
import org.springframework.beans.factory.annotation.Qualifier;
import org.springframework.ldap.core.DistinguishedName;
import org.springframework.ldap.odm.core.OdmManager;
import org.springframework.stereotype.Service;
import com.inflinx.book.ldap.domain.Patron;

@Service("patronService" )
public class PatronServiceImpl implements PatronService {
```

```java
    private static final String PATRON_BASE = "ou=patrons,dc=inflinx,dc=com";

    @Autowired
    @Qualifier("odmManager" )
    private OdmManager odmManager;

    @Override
    public void create(Patron patron) {
        odmManager.create(patron);
    }
    @Override
    public void update(Patron patron) {
        odmManager.update(patron);
    }
    @Override
    public Patron find(String id) {
        DistinguishedName dn = new DistinguishedName(PATRON_BASE);
        dn.add("uid", id);
        return odmManager.read(Patron.class, dn);
    }
    @Override
    public void delete(String id) {
        odmManager.delete(find(id));
    }
}
```

The JUnit test to verify the PatronService implementation is shown in Listing 8-16.

Listing 8-16.

```java
package com.inflinx.book.ldap.service;

import org.junit.After;
import org.junit.Before;
import org.junit.Test;
import org.junit.runner.RunWith;
import org.ldapunit.util.LdapUnitUtils;
import org.springframework.beans.factory.annotation.Autowired;
import org.springframework.core.io.ClassPathResource;
import org.springframework.ldap.NameNotFoundException;
import org.springframework.ldap.core.DistinguishedName;
import org.springframework.test.context.ContextConfiguration;
import org.springframework.test.context.junit4.SpringJUnit4ClassRunner;
import com.inflinx.book.ldap.domain.Patron;
import static org.junit.Assert.assertNotNull;
import static org.junit.Assert.assertEquals;
import static org.junit.Assert.assertNull;
```

```java
@RunWith(SpringJUnit4ClassRunner.class )
@ContextConfiguration("classpath:repositoryContext-test.xml" )
public class PatronServiceImplTest {

    @Autowired
    private PatronService patronService;
    private static final String PORT = "12389";
    private static final String ROOT_DN = "dc=inflinx,dc=com";

    @Before
    public void setup() throws Exception {
        System.out.println("Inside the setup");
        LdapUnitUtils.loadData(new ClassPathResource("patrons.ldif"), PORT);
    }

    @After
    public void teardown() throws Exception {
        System.out.println("Inside the teardown");
        LdapUnitUtils.clearSubContexts(new DistinguishedName(ROOT_DN), PORT);
    }

    @Test
    public void testService() {
        Patron patron = new Patron();

        patron.setDn(new DistinguishedName("uid=patron10001," + "ou=patrons,
        dc=inflinx,dc=com"));
        patron.setFirstName("Patron");
        patron.setLastName("Test 1");
        patron.setFullName("Patron Test 1");
        patron.setMail("balaji@inflinx.com" );
        patron.setEmployeeNumber(1234);
        patron.setTelephoneNumber("8018640759");
        patronService.create(patron);

        // Lets read the patron
        patron = patronService.find("patron10001");
        assertNotNull(patron);

        patron.setTelephoneNumber("8018640850");
        patronService.update(patron);
        patron = patronService.find("patron10001");
        assertEquals(patron.getTelephoneNumber(), "8018640850");
        patronService.delete("patron10001");
```

143

```
        try {
            patron = patronService.find("patron10001");
            assertNull(patron);
        }
        catch(NameNotFoundException e) {
        }
    }
}
```

The repositoryContext-test.xml file contains snippets of the configuration you have seen so far. Listing 8-17 gives the complete content of the XML file.

Listing 8-17.

```xml
<?xml version="1.0" encoding="UTF-8"?>
<beans xmlns="http://www.springframework.org/schema/beans"
xmlns:xsi="http://www.w3.org/2001/XMLSchema-instance"
xmlns:context="http://www.springframework.org/schema/context"
xsi:schemaLocation="http://www.springframework.org/schema/beans
http://www.springframework.org/schema/beans/spring-beans.xsd
http://www.springframework.org/schema/context
http://www.springframework.org/schema/context/spring-context.xsd">

    <context:component-scan base-package="com.inflinx.book.ldap" />
    <bean id="contextSource" class="org.ldapunit.context.
EmbeddedContextSourceFactory">
        <property name="port" value="12389" />
        <property name="rootDn" value="dc=inflinx,dc=com" />
        <property name="serverType" value="OPENDJ" />
    </bean>
    <bean id="odmManager" class="org.springframework.ldap.odm.core.impl.
OdmManagerImpl">
        <constructor-arg name="converterManager" ref="converterManager" />
        <constructor-arg name="contextSource" ref="contextSource" />
        <constructor-arg name="managedClasses">
            <set>
                <value>com.inflinx.book.ldap.domain.Patron</value>
            </set>
        </constructor-arg>
    </bean>
    <bean id="fromStringConverter" class="org.springframework.ldap.odm.
typeconversion.impl.converters.FromStringConverter" />
    <bean id="toStringConverter" class="org.springframework.ldap.odm.
typeconversion.impl.converters.ToStringConverter" />

    <!-- Configuration information for a single instance of FromString -->
    <bean id="fromStringConverterConfig" class="org.springframework.ldap.odm.
typeconversion.impl.ConverterManagerFactoryBean$ConverterConfig">
```

```xml
            <property name="converter" ref="fromStringConverter" />
            <property name="fromClasses">
                <set>
                    <value>java.lang.String</value>
                </set>
            </property>
            <property name="toClasses">
                <set>
                    <value>java.lang.Byte</value>
                    <value>java.lang.Integer</value>
                    <value>java.lang.Boolean</value>
                </set>
            </property>
        </bean>
        <bean id="toStringCoverterConfig" class="org.springframework.ldap.odm.
        typeconversion.impl.ConverterManagerFactoryBean$ConverterConfig">
            <property name="converter" ref="toStringConverter" />
            <property name="fromClasses">
                <set>
                    <value>java.lang.Byte</value>
                    <value>java.lang.Integer</value>
                    <value>java.lang.Boolean</value>
                </set>
            </property>
            <property name="toClasses">
                <set>
                    <value>java.lang.String</value>
                </set>
            </property>
        </bean>
        <bean id="converterManager" class="org.springframework.ldap.odm.
        typeconversion.impl.ConverterManagerFactoryBean">
            <property name="converterConfig">
                <set>
                    <ref bean="fromStringConverterConfig"/>
                    <ref bean="toStringCoverterConfig"/>
                </set>
            </property>
        </bean>
</beans>
```

Configuration Simplifications

The configuration in Listing 8-17 may look daunting at first. So to address this, let's create
a new ConverterManager implementation that simplifies the configuration process.
Listing 8-18 shows the DefaultConverterManagerImpl class. As you can see, it uses the
ConverterManagerImpl class internal to its implementation.

145

Listing 8-18.

```
package com.inflinx.book.ldap.converter;

import org.springframework.ldap.odm.typeconversion.ConverterManager;
import org.springframework.ldap.odm.typeconversion.impl.Converter;
import org.springframework.ldap.odm.typeconversion.impl.
ConverterManagerImpl;
import org.springframework.ldap.odm.typeconversion.impl.converters.
FromStringConverter;
import org.springframework.ldap.odm.typeconversion.impl.converters.
ToStringConverter;

public class DefaultConverterManagerImpl implements ConverterManager {

    private static final Class[] classSet = { java.lang.Byte.class, java.
    lang.Integer.class, java.lang.Long.class, java.lang.Double.class, java.
    lang.Boolean.class };
    private ConverterManagerImpl converterManager;

    public DefaultConverterManagerImpl() {
        converterManager = new ConverterManagerImpl();
        Converter fromStringConverter = new FromStringConverter();
        Converter toStringConverter = new ToStringConverter();
        for(Class clazz : classSet) {
            converterManager.addConverter(String.class, null, clazz,
            fromStringConverter);
            converterManager.addConverter(clazz, null, String.class,
            toStringConverter);
        }
    }

    @Override
    public boolean canConvert(Class<?> fromClass, String syntax, Class<?> toClass) {
        return converterManager.canConvert(fromClass, syntax, toClass);
    }

    @Override
    public <T> T convert(Object source, String syntax, Class<T> toClass) {
        return converterManager.convert(source,syntax,toClass);
    }
}
```

Using this class reduces the needed configuration quite a bit, as shown in Listing 8-19.

Listing 8-19.

```
<?xml version="1.0" encoding="UTF-8"?>
<beans xmlns="http://www.springframework.org/schema/beans"
xmlns:xsi="http://www.w3.org/2001/XMLSchema-instance"
xmlns:context="http://www.springframework.org/schema/context"
xsi:schemaLocation="http://www.springframework.org/schema/beans
http://www.springframework.org/schema/beans/spring-beans.xsd
http://www.springframework.org/schema/context
http://www.springframework.org/schema/context/spring-context.xsd">

    <context:component-scan base-package="com.inflinx.book.ldap" />
    <bean id="contextSource" class="org.ldapunit.context.
    EmbeddedContextSourceFactory">
        <property name="port" value="12389" />
        <property name="rootDn" value="dc=inflinx,dc=com" />
        <property name="serverType" value="OPENDJ" />
    </bean>
    <bean id="odmManager" class="org.springframework.ldap.odm.core.impl.
    OdmManagerImplFactoryBean">
        <property name="converterManager" ref="converterManager" />
        <property name="contextSource" ref="contextSource" />
        <property name="managedClasses">
            <set>
                <value>com.inflinx.book.ldap.domain.Patron</value>
            </set>
        </property>
    </bean>
    <bean id="converterManager" class="com.inflinx.book.ldap.converter.
    DefaultConverterManagerImpl" />
</beans>
```

Creating Custom Converter

Consider the scenario where your Patron class uses a custom PhoneNumber class for storing a patron's phone number. Now, when a Patron class needs to be persisted, you need to convert the PhoneNumber class to String type. Similarly, when you read a Patron class from LDAP, the data in the telephone attribute needs to be converted into PhoneNumber class. The default ToStringConverter and FromStringConverter will not be useful for such conversion. Listing 8-20 and Listing 8-21 show the PhoneNumber and modified Patron classes, respectively.

Listing 8-20.

```java
package com.inflinx.book.ldap.custom;

public class PhoneNumber {

    private int areaCode;
    private int exchange;
    private int extension;

    public PhoneNumber(int areaCode, int exchange, int extension) {
        this.areaCode = areaCode;
        this.exchange = exchange;
        this.extension = extension;
    }

    public boolean equals(Object obj) {
        if(obj == null || obj.getClass() != this.getClass())
        { return false; }

        PhoneNumber p = (PhoneNumber) obj;
            return (this.areaCode == p.areaCode) && (this.exchange ==
            p.exchange) && (this.extension == p.extension);
    }

    public String toString() {
        return String.format("+1 %03d %03d %04d", areaCode, exchange,
        extension);
    }

    // satisfies the hashCode contract
    public int hashCode() {
        int result = 17;
        result = 37 * result + areaCode;
        result = 37 * result + exchange;
        result = 37 * result + extension;

            return result;
    }
}
```

Listing 8-21.

```java
package com.inflinx.book.ldap.custom;

import java.util.List;
import javax.naming.Name;
```

```java
import org.springframework.ldap.odm.annotations.Attribute;
import org.springframework.ldap.odm.annotations.Entry;
import org.springframework.ldap.odm.annotations.Id;

@Entry(objectClasses = { "inetorgperson", "organizationalperson", "person", "top" })
public class Patron {

    @Id
    private Name dn;

    @Attribute(name = "sn")
    private String lastName;

    @Attribute(name = "givenName")
    private String firstName;

    @Attribute(name = "telephoneNumber")
    private PhoneNumber phoneNumber;

    @Attribute(name = "cn")
    private String fullName;
    private String mail;

    @Attribute(name = "objectClass")
    private List<String> objectClasses;

    @Attribute(name = "employeeNumber", syntax = "2.16.840.1.113730.3.1.3")
     private int employeeNumber;

    // Getters and setters

    @Override
    public String toString() {
        return "Dn: " + dn + ", firstName: " + firstName + "," + " fullName: "
        + fullName + ", " + "Telephone Number: " + phoneNumber;
    }
}
```

To convert PhoneNumber to String, you create a new FromPhoneNumberConverter converter. Listing 8-22 shows the implementation. The implementation simply involves calling the toString method to perform the conversion.

Listing 8-22.

```java
package com.inflinx.book.ldap.custom;

import org.springframework.ldap.odm.typeconversion.impl.Converter;

public class FromPhoneNumberConverter implements Converter {
```

```java
    @Override
    public <T> T convert(Object source, Class<T> toClass) throws Exception {
        T result = null;
        if(PhoneNumber.class.isAssignableFrom(source.getClass()) && toClass.
        equals(String.class)) {
            result = toClass.cast(source.toString());
        }
        return result;
    }
}
```

Next, you need an implementation to convert the LDAP string attribute to Java
PhoneNumber type. To do this, you create the ToPhoneNumberConverter, as shown in
Listing 8-23.

Listing 8-23.

```java
package com.inflinx.book.ldap.custom;

import org.springframework.ldap.odm.typeconversion.impl.Converter;

public class ToPhoneNumberConverter implements  Converter {

    @Override
    public <T> T convert(Object source, Class<T> toClass) throws Exception {
        T result = null;
        if(String.class.isAssignableFrom(source.getClass()) && toClass ==
        PhoneNumber.class) {
        // Simple implementation
        String[] tokens = ((String)source).split(" ");
        int i = 0;
        if(tokens.length == 4) {
            i = 1;
        }
        result = toClass.cast(new PhoneNumber(
            Integer.parseInt(tokens[i]),
            Integer.parseInt(tokens[i+1]),
            Integer.parseInt(tokens[i+2])));
        }
        return result;
    }
}
```

Finally, you tie up everything in the configuration, as shown in Listing 8-24.

Listing 8-24.

```xml
<?xml version="1.0" encoding="UTF-8"?>
<beans xmlns="http://www.springframework.org/schema/beans"
xmlns:xsi="http://www.w3.org/2001/XMLSchema-instance"
xmlns:context="http://www.springframework.org/schema/context"
xsi:schemaLocation="http://www.springframework.org/schema/beans
http://www.springframework.org/schema/beans/spring-beans.xsd
http://www.springframework.org/schema/context
http://www.springframework.org/schema/context/spring-context.xsd">

    <context:component-scan base-package="com.inflinx.book.ldap" />
    <bean id="contextSource" class="org.ldapunit.context.
EmbeddedContextSourceFactory">
        <property name="port" value="12389" />
        <property name="rootDn" value="dc=inflinx,dc=com" />
        <property name="serverType" value="OPENDJ" />
    </bean>
    <bean id="odmManager" class="org.springframework.ldap.odm.core.impl.
    OdmManagerImpl">
        <constructor-arg name="converterManager" ref="converterManager" />
        <constructor-arg name="contextSource" ref="contextSource" />
        <constructor-arg name="managedClasses">
           <set>
              <value>com.inflinx.book.ldap.custom.Patron</value>
           </set>
        </constructor-arg>
    </bean>
    <bean id="fromStringConverter" class="org.springframework.ldap.odm.
    typeconversion.impl.converters.FromStringConverter" />
    <bean id="toStringConverter" class="org.springframework.ldap.odm.
    typeconversion.impl.converters.ToStringConverter" />
    <bean id="fromPhoneNumberConverter" class="com.inflinx.book.ldap.custom.
    FromPhoneNumberConverter" />
    <bean id="toPhoneNumberConverter" class="com.inflinx.book.ldap.custom.
    ToPhoneNumberConverter" />

    <!-- Configuration information for a single instance of FromString -->
    <bean id="fromStringConverterConfig" class="org.springframework.ldap.odm.
    typeconversion.impl.ConverterManagerFactoryBean$ConverterConfig">
        <property name="converter" ref="fromStringConverter" />
        <property name="fromClasses">
          <set>
             <value>java.lang.String</value>
          </set>
        </property>
```

```xml
    <property name="toClasses">
      <set>
         <value>java.lang.Byte</value>
         <value>java.lang.Integer</value>
         <value>java.lang.Boolean</value>
      </set>
   </property>
</bean>
<bean id="fromPhoneNumberConverterConfig" class="org.springframework.
ldap.odm.typeconversion.impl.ConverterManagerFactoryBean$ConverterConfig">
   <property name="converter" ref="fromPhoneNumberConverter" />
   <property name="fromClasses">
      <set>
         <value>com.inflinx.book.ldap.custom.PhoneNumber</value>
      </set>
   </property>
   <property name="toClasses">
      <set>
         <value>java.lang.String</value>
      </set>
   </property>
</bean>
<bean id="toPhoneNumberConverterConfig" class="org.springframework.ldap.
odm.typeconversion.impl.ConverterManagerFactoryBean$ConverterConfig">
   <property name="converter" ref="toPhoneNumberConverter" />
   <property name="fromClasses">
      <set>
         <value>java.lang.String</value>
      </set>
   </property>
   <property name="toClasses">
      <set>
         <value>com.inflinx.book.ldap.custom.PhoneNumber</value>
      </set>
   </property>
</bean>
<bean id="toStringConverterConfig" class="org.springframework.ldap.odm.
typeconversion.impl.ConverterManagerFactoryBean$ConverterConfig">
   <property name="converter" ref="toStringConverter"/>
   <property name="fromClasses">
      <set>
         <value>java.lang.Byte</value>
         <value>java.lang.Integer</value>
         <value>java.lang.Boolean</value>
      </set>
   </property>
```

```xml
        <property name="toClasses">
           <set>
              <value>java.lang.String</value>
           </set>
        </property>
     </bean>
     <bean id="converterManager" class="org.springframework.ldap.odm.
     typeconversion.impl.ConverterManagerFactoryBean">
        <property name="converterConfig">
           <set>
              <ref bean="fromPhoneNumberConverterConfig"/>
              <ref bean="toPhoneNumberConverterConfig"/>
              <ref bean="fromStringConverterConfig"/>
              <ref bean="toStringConverterConfig"/>
           </set>
        </property>
     </bean>
</beans>
```

The modified test case for testing the newly added converters is shown in
Listing 8-25.

Listing 8-25.

```java
@RunWith(SpringJUnit4ClassRunner.class )
@ContextConfiguration("classpath:repositoryContext-test3.xml")
public class PatronServiceImplCustomTest {

   @Autowired
   private PatronService patronService;
   private static final String PORT = "12389";
   private static final String ROOT_DN = "dc=inflinx,dc=com";

   @Before
   public void setup() throws Exception {
      System.out.println("Inside the setup");
      LdapUnitUtils.loadData(new ClassPathResource("patrons.ldif"), PORT);
   }

   @After
   public void teardown() throws Exception {
      System.out.println("Inside the teardown");
      LdapUnitUtils.clearSubContexts(new DistinguishedName(ROOT_DN), PORT);
   }
```

```
@Test
public void testService() {
    Patron patron = new Patron();
    patron.setDn(new DistinguishedName("uid=patron10001," + "ou=patrons,
    dc=inflinx,dc=com"));
    patron.setFirstName("Patron"); patron.setLastName("Test 1");
    patron.setFullName("Patron Test 1");
    patron.setMail("balaji@inflinx.com" );
    patron.setEmployeeNumber(1234);
    patron.setPhoneNumber(new PhoneNumber(801, 864, 8050));
    patronService.create(patron);

    // Lets read the patron
    patron = patronService.find("patron10001");
    assertNotNull(patron);

        System.out.println(patron.getPhoneNumber());
    patron.setPhoneNumber(new PhoneNumber(435, 757, 9369));
    patronService.update(patron);

        System.out.println("updated phone: " + patron.getPhoneNumber());
    patron = patronService.find("patron10001");

        System.out.println("Read the phone number: " + patron.getPhoneNumber());
    assertEquals(patron.getPhoneNumber(), new PhoneNumber(435, 757, 9369));

        patronService.delete("patron10001");
    try {
        patron = patronService.find("patron10001");
        assertNull(patron);
    }
    catch(NameNotFoundException e) {
    }
}
}
```

Summary

Spring LDAP's Object-Directory Mapping (ODM) bridges the gap between object
and directory models. In this chapter, you learned the basics of ODM and looked at
annotations for defining ODM mappings. You then took a deep dive into the ODM
framework and built a Patron service and custom converters.

Up to this point in the book, you have created several variations of Service and
DAO implementations. In the next chapter, you will explore Spring LDAP's support for
transactions.

CHAPTER 9

■ ■ ■

LDAP Transactions

In this chapter, you will learn

- The basics of transactions.
- Spring transaction abstraction.
- Spring LDAP support for transactions.

Transaction Basics

Transactions are an integral part of enterprise applications. Put simply, a transaction is a series of operations that are performed together. For a transaction to be completed or committed, all its operations must succeed. If, for any reason, one operation fails, the entire transaction fails and is rolled back. In that scenario, all the previous operations that have succeeded must be undone. This ensures that the end state matches the state that was in place before the transaction started.

In your day-to-day world, you run into transactions all the time. Consider an online banking scenario where you wish to transfer $300 from your savings account to your checking account. This operation involves debiting the savings account by $300 and crediting the checking account by $300. If the debiting part of the operation were to succeed and the crediting part fail, you would end up with $300 less in your combined accounts. (Ideally, we all would like the debit operation to fail and the credit operation to succeed, but the bank might be knocking on our door the next day.) Banks ensure that accounts never end up in such inconsistent states by using transactions.

Transactions are usually associated with the following four well-known characteristics, often referred to as ACID properties:

- **Atomicity:** This property ensures that a transaction executes completely or not at all. So in our above example, we either successfully transfer the money or our transfer fails. This all-or-nothing property is also referred to as single unit of work or logical unit of work.

- **Consistency:** This property ensures that a transaction leaves the system in a consistent state after its completion. For example, with a database system, this means that all the integrity constraints, such as primary key or referential integrity, are satisfied.

155

- **Isolation:** This property ensures that a transaction executes independent of other parallel transactions. Changes or side effects of a transaction that has not yet completed will never be seen by other transactions. In the money transfer scenario, another owner of the account will only see the balances before or after the transfer. They will never be able to see the intermediate balances no matter how long the transaction takes to complete. Many database systems relax this property and provide several levels of isolation. Table 9-1 lists the primary transaction levels and descriptions. As the isolation level increases, transaction concurrency decreases and transaction consistency increases.

Table 9-1. Isolation Levels

Isolation Level	Description
Read Uncommitted	This isolation level allows a running transaction to see changes made by other uncommitted transactions. Changes made by this transaction become visible to other transactions even before it completes. This is the lowest level of isolation and can more appropriately be considered as lack of isolation. Since it completely violates one of the ACID properties, it is not supported by most database vendors.
Read Committed	This isolation level allows a query in a running transaction to see only data committed before the query began. However, all uncommitted changes or changes committed by concurrent transactions during query execution will not be seen. This is the default isolation level for most databases including Oracle, MySQL, and PostgreSQL.
Repeatable Read	This isolation level allows a query in a running transaction to read the same data every time it is executed. To achieve this, the transaction acquires locks on all the rows examined (not just fetched) until it is complete.
Serializable	This is the strictest and most expensive of all the isolation levels. Interleaving transactions are stacked up so that transactions are executed one after another rather than concurrently. With this isolation level, queries will only see the data that has been committed before the start of the transaction and will never see uncommitted changes or commits by concurrent transactions.

- **Durability:** This property ensures that the results of a committed transaction never get lost due to a failure. Revisiting the bank transfer scenario, when you receive a confirmation that the transfer has succeeded, the durability property makes sure that this change becomes permanent.

Local vs. Global Transactions

Transactions are often categorized into either local or global transactions depending on the number of resources that participate in the transaction. Examples of these resources include a database system or a JMS queue. Resource managers such as a JDBC driver are typically used to manage resources.

Local transactions are transactions that involve a single resource. The most common example is a transaction associated with a single database. These transactions are usually managed via objects used to access the resource. In the case of a JDBC database transaction, implementations of the `java.sql.Connection` interface are used to access the database. These implementations also provide `commit` and `rollback` methods for managing transactions. In the case of a JMS queue, the `javax.jms.Session` instance provides methods for controlling transactions.

Global transactions, on the other hand, deal with multiple resources. For example, a global transaction can be used to read a message from a JMS queue and write a record to the database all in one transaction.

Global transactions are managed using a transaction manager that is external to the resources. It is responsible for communicating with resource managers and making the final commit or rollback decision on distributed transactions. In Java/JEE, global transactions are implemented using Java Transaction API (JTA). JTA provides standard interfaces for transaction manager and transaction participating components.

Transaction managers employ a "two phase commit" protocol to coordinate global transactions. As the names suggests, the two phase commit protocol has the following two phases:

- **Prepare phase:** In this phase, all participating resource managers are asked if they are ready to commit their work. Upon receiving the request, the resource managers attempt to record their state. If successful, the resource manager responds positively. If it cannot commit, the resource manager responds negatively and rolls back the local changes.

- **Commit phase:** If the transaction manager receives all positive responses, it commits the transaction and notifies all the participants of the commit. If it receives one or more negative responses, it rolls back the entire transaction and notifies all the participants.

The two phase commit protocol is shown in Figure 9-1.

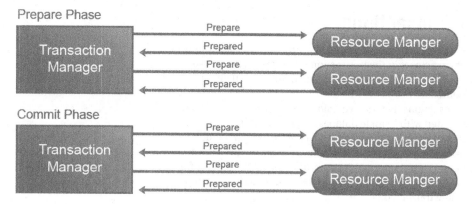

Figure 9-1. *Two phase commit protocol*

Programmatic vs. Declarative Transactions

Developers have two choices when it comes to adding transaction capabilities to their application.

Programmatically

In this scenario, the transaction management code for starting, committing, or rolling back transactions surrounds the business code. This can provide extreme flexibility but can also make maintenance difficult. The following code gives an example of programmatic transaction using JTA and EJB 3.0:

```
@Stateless
@TransactionManagement(TransactionManagementType.BEAN)
public class OrderManager {

    @Resource
    private UserTransaction transaction;

    public void create(Order order) {
    try {
       transaction.begin();
       // business logic for processing order
       verifyAddress(order);
           processOrder(order);
       sendConfirmation(order);
       transaction.commit();
    }
```

```
        catch(Exception e) {
            transaction.rollback();
        }
    }
}
```

Declaratively

In this scenario, the container is responsible for starting, committing, or rolling back transactions. The developer usually specifies the transaction behavior via annotations or XML. This model cleanly separates the transaction management code from business logic. The following code gives an example of declarative transactions using JTA and EJB 3.0. When an exception happens during order processing, the setRollbackOnly method on the session context is called; this marks that the transaction must be rolled back.

```
@Stateless
@TransactionManagement(TransactionManagementType.CONTAINER)
public class OrderManager {

    @Resource
    private SessionContext context;

    @TransactionAttribute(TransactionAttributeType.REQUIRED)
    public void create(Order order) {
    try {
        // business logic for processing order
        verifyAddress(order);
            processOrder(order);
        sendConfirmation(order);
    }
    catch(Exception e) {
        context.setRollbackOnly();
    }
    }
}
```

Spring Transaction Abstraction

The Spring Framework provides a consistent programming model for handling both global and local transactions. The transaction abstraction hides the inner workings of different transaction APIs, such as JTA, JDBC, JMS, and JPA, and allows developers to write transaction-enabled code in an environment-neutral way. Behind the scenes, Spring simply delegates the transaction management to the underlying transaction providers. Both programmatic and declarative transaction management models are supported without requiring any EJBs. The declarative approach is usually recommended and that is what we will be using in this book.

Central to Spring's transaction management is the PlatformTransactionManager abstraction. It exposes key aspects of transaction management in a technology-independent manner. It is responsible for creating and managing transactions and is required for both declarative and programmatic transactions. Several implementations of this interface, such as JtaTransactionManager, DataSourceTransactionManager and JmsTransactionManager, are available out of the box. The PlatformTransactionManager API is shown in Listing 9-1.

Listing 9-1.

```
package org.springframework.transaction;

public interface PlatformTransactionManager {

    TransactionStatus getTransaction(TransactionDefinition definition) throws
    TransactionException;
    void commit(TransactionStatus status) throws TransactionException;
    void rollback(TransactionStatus status) throws TransactionException;
    String getName();
}
```

The getTransaction method in the PlatformTransactionManager is used to retrieve an existing transaction. If no active transaction is found, this method might create a new transaction based on the transactional properties specified in the TransactionDefinition instance. The following is the list of properties that TransactionDefinition interface abstracts:

- **Read-only:** This property indicates whether this transaction is read-only or not.

- **Timeout:** This property mandates the time in which the transaction must complete. If the transaction fails to complete in the specified time, it will be rolled back automatically.

- **Isolation:** This property controls the degree of isolation among transactions. The possible isolation levels are discussed in Table 9-1.

- **Propagation:** Consider the scenario where an active transaction exists and Spring encounters code that needs to be executed in a transaction. One option in that scenario is to execute the code in the existing transaction. Another option is to suspend the existing transaction and start a new transaction to execute the code. The propagation property can be used to define such transaction behavior. Possible values include PROPAGATION_REQUIRED, PROPAGATION_REQUIRES_NEW, PROPAGATION_SUPPORTS, etc.

The getTransaction method returns an instance of TransactionStatus representing the status of the current transaction. Application code can use this interface to check if this is a new transaction or if the transaction has been completed. The interface can also be used to programmatically request a transaction rollback. The other two methods in the PlatformTransactionManager are commit and rollback which, as their names suggest, can be used to commit or roll back the transaction.

Declarative Transactions Using Spring

Spring provides two ways to declaratively add transaction behavior to applications: pure XML and annotations. The annotation approach is very popular and greatly simplifies the configuration. To demonstrate declarative transactions, consider the simple scenario of inserting a new record in a Person table in a database. Listing 9-2 gives the PersonRepositoryImpl class with a create method implementing this scenario.

Listing 9-2.

```
import org.springframework.jdbc.core.JdbcTemplate;

public class PersonRepositoryImpl implements PersonRepository {

    private JdbcTemplate jdbcTemplate;

    public void create(String firstName, String lastName) {
        String sql = "INSERT INTO PERSON (FIRST_NAME, " + "LAST_NAME) VALUES (?, ?)";
        jdbcTemplate.update(sql, new Object[]{firstName, lastName});
    }
}
```

Listing 9-3 shows the PersonRepository interface that the above class implements.

Listing 9-3.

```
public interface PersonRepository {

    public void create(String firstName, String lastName);

}
```

The next step is to make the create method transactional. This is done by simply annotating the method with @Transactional, as shown in Listing 9-4. (Note that I annotated the method in the implementation and not the method in the interface.)

Listing 9-4.

```
import org.springframework.transaction.annotation.Transactional;

public class PersonRepositoryImpl implements PersonRepository {
    ...........
    @Transactional
    public void create(String firstName, String lastName) {
    ...........
    }
}
```

The @Transactional annotation has several properties that can be used to specify additional information such as propagation and isolation. Listing 9-5 shows the method with default isolation and REQUIRES_NEW propagation.

Listing 9-5.

```
@Transactional(propagation=Propagation.REQUIRES_NEW, isolation=Isolation.DEFAULT)
public void create(String  firstName, String lastName) {
}
```

The next step is to specify a transaction manager for Spring to use. Since you are going after a single database, the org.springframework.jdbc.datasource.DataSourc eTransactionManager shown in Listing 9-6 is ideal for your case. From Listing 9-6, you can see that the DataSourceTransactionManager needs a datasource in order to obtain and manage connections to the database.

Listing 9-6.

```
<bean id="transactionManager" class="org.springframework.jdbc.datasource.
DataSourceTransactionManager">
    <property name="dataSource" ref="dataSource"/>
</bean>
```

The complete application context configuration file for declarative transaction management is given in Listing 9-7.

Listing 9-7.

```
<?xml version="1.0" encoding="UTF-8"?>
<beans xmlns="http://www.springframework.org/schema/beans"
xmlns:xsi="http://www.w3.org/2001/XMLSchema-instance"
xmlns:context="http://www.springframework.org/schema/context"
xmlns:tx="http://www.springframework.org/schema/tx"
```

```
xmlns:aop="http://www.springframework.org/schema/aop"
xsi:schemaLocation="http://www.springframework.org/schema/beans
http://www.springframework.org/schema/beans/spring-beans.xsd
http://www.springframework.org/schema/context
http://www.springframework.org/schema/context/spring-context.xsd
http://www.springframework.org/schema/tx
http://www.springframework.org/schema/tx/spring-tx.xsd
http://www.springframework.org/schema/aop
http://www.springframework.org/schema/tx/spring-aop.xsd">

    <bean id="transactionManager" class="org.springframework.jdbc.datasource.
    DataSourceTransactionManager">
        <property name="dataSource" ref="dataSource"/>
    </bean>
    <tx:annotation-driven transaction-manager="transactionManager"/>
    <aop:aspectj-autoproxy />
</beans>
```

The `<tx:annotation-driven/>` tag indicates that you are using annotation-based transaction management. This tag, along with `<aop:aspectj-autoproxy />`, instructs Spring to use Aspect-Oriented Programming (AOP) and create proxies that manage transaction on behalf of the annotated class. So, when a call is made to a transactional method, the proxy intercepts the call and uses the transaction manager to obtain a transaction (new or existing). The called method is then invoked, and if the method completes successfully, the proxy using the transaction manager will commit the transaction. If the method fails, throwing an exception, the transaction will be rolled back. This AOP-based transaction processing is shown in Figure 9-2.

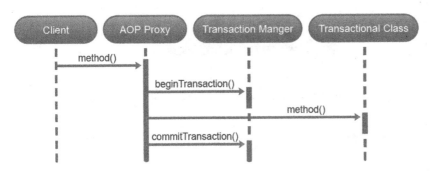

Figure 9-2. *AOP-based Spring transaction*

LDAP Transaction Support

The LDAP protocol requires that all LDAP operations (such as modify or delete) follow ACID properties. This transactional behavior ensures consistency of the information stored in the LDAP server. However, LDAP does not define transactions across multiple operations. Consider the scenario where you want to add two LDAP entries as one atomic operation. A successful completion of the operation means that both entries get added to the LDAP server. If there is a failure and one of the entries can't be added, the server will automatically undo the addition of the other entry. Such transactional behavior is not part of the LDAP specification and does not exist in the world of LDAP. Also, the lack of transactional semantics such as commit and rollback make it impossible to assure data consistency across multiple LDAP servers.

Though transactions are not part of the LDAP specification, servers such as IBM Tivoli Directory Server and ApacheDS provide transaction support. The Begin transaction (OID 1.3.18.0.2.12.5) and End transaction (OID 1.3.18.0.2.12.6) extended controls supported by IBM Tivoli Directory Server can be used to demarcate a set of operations inside a transaction. The RFC 5805 (`http://tools.ietf.org/html/rfc5805`) attempts to standardize transactions in LDAP and is currently in experimental state.

Spring LDAP Transaction Support

The lack of transactions in LDAP might seem surprising at first. More importantly, it can act as a barrier to the widespread adoption of directory servers in enterprises. To address this, Spring LDAP offers a non-LDAP/JNDI-specific compensating transaction support. This transaction support integrates tightly with the Spring transaction management infrastructure you saw in the earlier section. Figure 9-3 shows the components responsible for Spring LDAP transaction support.

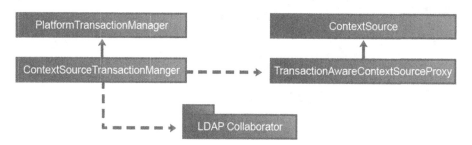

Figure 9-3. *Spring LDAP transaction support*

The ContextSourceTransactionManager class implements PlatformTransactionManager and is responsible for managing LDAP-based transactions. This class, along with its collaborators, keeps track of the LDAP operations performed inside the transaction and makes a record of the state before each operation. If the transaction were to rollback, the transaction manager will take steps to restore the original state. To achieve this behavior, the transaction manager uses a TransactionAwareContextSourceProxy instead of working directly with LdapContextSource. This proxy class also ensures that a single javax.naming.directory.DirContext instance is used throughout the transaction and will not be closed until the transaction is finished.

Compensating Transactions

A compensating transaction undoes the effects of a previously committed transaction and restores the system to a previous consistent state. Consider a transaction that involves booking an airline ticket. A compensating transaction in that scenario is an operation that cancels the reservation. In the case of LDAP, if an operation adds a new LDAP entry, the corresponding compensating transaction simply involves removing that entry.

Compensating transactions are useful for resources such as LDAP and web services that don't provide any standard transactional support. However, it is important to remember that compensating transactions provide an illusion and can never replace real transactions. So, if a server crashes or the connection to the LDAP server is lost before the compensating transaction completes, you will end up with inconsistent data. Also, since the transaction is already committed, concurrent transactions might see invalid data. Compensating transactions can result in additional overhead as the client has to deal with extra undo operations.

To understand Spring LDAP transactions better, let's create a Patron service with transactional behavior. Listing 9-8 shows the PatronService interface with just a create method.

Listing 9-8.

```
package com.inflinx.book.ldap.transactions;

import com.inflinx.book.ldap.domain.Patron;

public interface PatronService {
    public void create(Patron patron);
}
```

Listing 9-9 shows the implementation of this service interface. The create method implementation simply delegates the call to the DAO layer.

Listing 9-9.

```
package com.inflinx.book.ldap.transactions;

import org.springframework.beans.factory.annotation.Autowired;
import org.springframework.beans.factory.annotation.Qualifier;
import org.springframework.stereotype.Service;
import org.springframework.transaction.annotation.Transactional;
import com.inflinx.book.ldap.domain.Patron;
```

```java
@Service("patronService")
@Transactional
public class PatronServiceImpl implements PatronService {

    @Autowired
    @Qualifier("patronDao")
    private PatronDao patronDao;

    @Override
    public void create(Patron patron) {
        patronDao.create(patron);
    }
}
```

Notice the usage of @Transactional annotation at the top of the class declaration. Listing 9-10 and Listing 9-11 show the PatronDao interface and its implementation PatronDaoImpl, respectively.

Listing 9-10.

```java
package com.inflinx.book.ldap.transactions;

import com.inflinx.book.ldap.domain.Patron;

public interface PatronDao {
    public void create(Patron patron);
}
```

Listing 9-11.

```java
package com.inflinx.book.ldap.transactions;

import org.springframework.beans.factory.annotation.Autowired;
import org.springframework.beans.factory.annotation.Qualifier;
import org.springframework.ldap.core.DirContextAdapter;
import org.springframework.ldap.core.DirContextOperations;
import org.springframework.ldap.core.DistinguishedName;
import org.springframework.ldap.core.LdapTemplate;
import org.springframework.stereotype.Repository;
import com.inflinx.book.ldap.domain.Patron;

@Repository("patronDao")
public class PatronDaoImpl implements PatronDao {

    private static final String PATRON_BASE = "ou=patrons,dc=inflinx,dc=com";
```

```
@Autowired
@Qualifier("ldapTemplate")
private LdapTemplate ldapTemplate;

@Override
public void create(Patron patron) {
    System.out.println("Inside the create method ...");
    DistinguishedName dn = new DistinguishedName(PATRON_BASE);
    dn.add("uid", patron.getUserId());
    DirContextAdapter context = new DirContextAdapter(dn);
    context.setAttributeValues("objectClass", new String[]
            {"top", "uidObject", "person", "organizationalPerson",
            "inetOrgPerson"});
    context.setAttributeValue("sn", patron.getLastName());
    context.setAttributeValue("cn", patron.getCn());
    ldapTemplate.bind(context);
}
}
```

As you can see from these two listings, you create Patron DAO and its implementation following the concepts discussed in Chapter 5. The next step is to create a Spring configuration file that will autowire the components and will include the transaction semantics. Listing 9-12 gives the contents of the configuration file. Here you are using the locally installed OpenDJ LDAP server.

Listing 9-12.

```
<?xml version="1.0" encoding="UTF-8"?>
<beans xmlns="http://www.springframework.org/schema/beans"
xmlns:xsi="http://www.w3.org/2001/XMLSchema-instance"
xmlns:context="http://www.springframework.org/schema/context"
xmlns:tx="http://www.springframework.org/schema/tx"
xsi:schemaLocation="http://www.springframework.org/schema/beans
http://www.springframework.org/schema/beans/spring-beans.xsd
http://www.springframework.org/schema/context
http://www.springframework.org/schema/context/
spring-context.xsd http://www.springframework.org/schema/tx
http://www.springframework.org/schema/tx/spring-tx.xsd">

    <context:component-scan base-package="com.inflinx.book.ldap" />
    <bean id="contextSourceTarget" class="org.springframework.ldap.core.
    support.LdapContextSource">
        <property name="url" value="ldap://localhost:11389" />
        <property name="userDn" value="cn=Directory Manager" />
        <property name="password" value="opendj" />
        <property name="base" value=""/>
```

```
  </bean>
  <bean id="contextSource" class="org.springframework.ldap.transaction.
  compensating.manager. TransactionAwareContextSourceProxy">
      <constructor-arg ref="contextSourceTarget" />
  </bean>
  <bean id="ldapTemplate" class="org.springframework.ldap. core.
  LdapTemplate">
      <constructor-arg ref="contextSource" />
  </bean>
  <bean id="transactionManager" class="org.springframework.ldap.
  transaction.compensating.manager.ContextSourceTransactionManager">
      <property name="contextSource" ref="contextSource" />
  </bean>
      <tx:annotation-driven transaction-manager="transactionManager" />
  </beans>
```

In this configuration, you start by defining a new LdapContextSource and providing it with your LDAP information. Up to this point, you referred to this bean with the id contextSource and injected it for use by LdapTemplate. However, in this new configuration, you are calling it contextSourceTarget. You then configure an instance of TransactionAwareContextSourceProxy and inject the contextSource bean into it. This newly configured TransactionAwareContextSourceProxy bean has the id contextSource and is used by LdapTemplate. Finally, you configure the transaction manager using ContextSourceTransactionManager class. As discussed earlier, this configuration allows a single DirContext instance to be used during a single transaction, which in turn enables transaction commit/rollback.

With this information in place, let's verify if your create method and configuration behaves correctly during a transaction rollback. In order to simulate a transaction rollback, let's modify the create method in the PatronServiceImpl class to throw a RuntimeException, as shown:

```
@Override
public void create(Patron patron) {
    patronDao.create(patron);
    throw new RuntimeException(); // Will roll back the transaction
}
```

The next step in verifying the expected behavior is to write a test case that calls PatronServiceImpl's create method in order to create a new Patron. The test case is shown in Listing 9-13. The repositoryContext-test.xml file contains the XML configuration defined in Listing 9-12.

Listing 9-13.

```
package com.inflinx.book.ldap.transactions;

@RunWith(SpringJUnit4ClassRunner.class)
@ContextConfiguration("classpath:repositoryContext-test.xml")
public class PatronServiceImplTest {
```

```
@Autowired
private PatronService patronService;

@Test(expected=RuntimeException.class)
public void testCreate() {
    Patron patron = new Patron();
    patron.setUserId("patron10001");
    patron.setLastName("Patron10001");
    patron.setCn("Test Patron10001");
    patronService.create(patron);
}
}
```

When you run the test, Spring LDAP should create a new patron; then, upon rolling back the transaction, it would remove the newly created patron. The inner workings of Spring LDAP's compensating transactions can be seen by looking at OpenDJ log file. The log file is named *access* and is located in the OPENDJ_INSTALL\logs folder.

Listing 9-14 shows a portion of the log file for this create operation. You will notice that when the create method on the PatronDaoImpl gets invoked, an "ADD REQ" command is sent to the OpenDJ server to add the new Patron entry. When Spring LDAP rolls back the transaction, a new "DELETE REQ" command is sent to remove the entry.

Listing 9-14.

```
[14/Sep/2013:15:03:09 -0600] CONNECT conn=52 from=127.0.0.1:54792
to=127.0.0.1:11389 protocol=LDAP
[14/Sep/2013:15:03:09 -0600] BIND REQ conn=52 op=0 msgID=1 type=SIMPLE
dn="cn=Directory Manager"
[14/Sep/2013:15:03:09 -0600] BIND RES conn=52 op=0 msgID=1 result=0
authDN="cn=Directory Manager,cn=Root DNs,cn=config" etime=0
[14/Sep/2013:15:03:09 -0600] ADD REQ conn=52 op=1 msgID=2
dn="uid=patron10001,ou=patrons,dc=inflinx,dc=com"
[14/Sep/2013:15:03:09 -0600] ADD RES conn=52 op=1 msgID=2 result=0 etime=2
[14/Sep/2013:15:03:09 -0600] DELETE REQ conn=52 op=2 msgID=3
dn="uid=patron10001,ou=patrons,dc=inflinx,dc=com"
[14/Sep/2013:15:03:09 -0600] DELETE RES conn=52 op=2 msgID=3 result=0 etime=4
[14/Sep/2013:15:03:09 -0600] UNBIND REQ conn=52 op=3 msgID=4
[14/Sep/2013:15:03:09 -0600] DISCONNECT conn=52 reason="Client Unbind""
```

This test verified that Spring LDAP's compensating transaction infrastructure would automatically remove the newly added entry if the transaction were to roll back for any reason.

Now let's continue implementing the PatronServiceImpl methods and verify their transactional behaviors. Listing 9-15 and Listing 9-16 show the delete method added to the PatronService interface and PatronServiceImpl class, respectively. Again, the actual delete method implementation is straightforward and simply involves calling the PatronDaoImpl's delete method.

Listing 9-15.

```
public interface PatronDao {
    public void create(Patron patron);
    public void delete(String id) ;
}
```

Listing 9-16.

```
// Import and annotations remvoed for brevity
public class PatronServiceImpl implements PatronService {

    // Create method removed for brevity
    @Override
    public void delete(String id) {
        patronDao.delete(id);
    }
}
```

Listing 9-17 shows the PatronDaoImpl's delete method implementation.

Listing 9-17.

```
// Annotation and imports removed for brevity
public class PatronDaoImpl implements PatronDao {

    // Removed other methods for brevity
    @Override
    public void delete(String id) {
        DistinguishedName dn = new DistinguishedName(PATRON_BASE);
        dn.add("uid", id);
        ldapTemplate.unbind(dn);
    }
}
```

With this code in hand, let's write a test case that invokes your delete method in a transaction. Listing 9-18 shows the test case. The "uid=patron98" is an existing entry in your OpenDJ server and was created during the LDIF import in Chapter 3.

Listing 9-18.

```
@Test
public void testDeletePatron() {
    patronService.delete("uid=patron98");
}
```

When you run this test case and invoke the PatronServiceImpl's delete method in a transaction, Spring LDAP's transaction infrastructure simply renames the entry under a newly calculated temporary DN. Essentially, with a rename, Spring LDAP is moving your entry to a different location on the LDAP server. Upon a successful commit, the temporary entry is removed. On a rollback, the entry is renamed and thus will be moved from the temporary location to its original location.

Now, run the method and watch the *access* log under OpenDJ. Listing 9-19 shows the portion for the log file for the delete operation. Notice that the delete operation results in a "MODIFYDN REQ" command that renames the entry to be deleted. Upon a successful commit, the renamed entry is removed via "DELETE REQ" command.

Listing 9-19.

```
[[14/Sep/2013:16:21:56 -0600] CONNECT conn=54 from=127.0.0.1:54824
to=127.0.0.1:11389 protocol=LDAP
[14/Sep/2013:16:21:56 -0600] BIND REQ conn=54 op=0 msgID=1 type=SIMPLE
dn="cn=Directory Manager"
[14/Sep/2013:16:21:56 -0600] BIND RES conn=54 op=0 msgID=1 result=0
authDN="cn=Directory Manager,cn=Root DNs,cn=config" etime=1
[14/Sep/2013:16:21:56 -0600] MODIFYDN REQ conn=54 op=1 msgID=2
dn="uid=patron97,ou=patrons,dc=inflinx,dc=com" newRDN="uid=patron97_temp"
deleteOldRDN=true newSuperior="ou=patrons,dc=inflinx,dc=com
[14/Sep/2013:16:21:56 -0600] MODIFYDN RES conn=54 op=1 msgID=2 result=0
etime=4
[14/Sep/2013:16:21:56 -0600] DELETE REQ conn=54 op=2 msgID=3
dn="uid=patron97_temp,ou=patrons,dc=inflinx,dc=com"
[14/Sep/2013:16:21:56 -0600] DELETE RES conn=54 op=2 msgID=3 result=0
etime=2
[14/Sep/2013:16:21:56 -0600] UNBIND REQ conn=54 op=3 msgID=4
[14/Sep/2013:16:21:56 -0600] DISCONNECT conn=54 reason="Client Unbind"
```

Now, let's simulate a rollback for the delete method in the PatronServiceImpl class, as shown in Listing 9-20.

Listing 9-20.

```
public void delete(String id) {
    patronDao.delete(id);
    throw new RuntimeException(); // Need this to simulate a rollback
}
```

Now, let's update the test case with a new Patron Id that you know still exists in the OpenDJ server, as shown in Listing 9-21.

Listing 9-21.

```
@Test(expected=RuntimeException.class)
public void testDeletePatron() {
    patronService.delete("uid=patron96");
}
```

When this code is run, the expected behavior is that Spring LDAP will rename the patron96 entry by changing its DN and then upon rollback will rename it again to the right DN. Listing 9-22 shows the OpenDJ's *access* log for the above operation. Note that the delete operation first results in renaming of the entry by sending the first MODIFYDN REQ. Upon a rollback, a second "MODIFYDN REQ" is sent to rename the entry back to original location.

Listing 9-22.

```
[14/Sep/2013:16:33:43 -0600] CONNECT conn=55 from=127.0.0.1:54829
to=127.0.0.1:11389 protocol=LDAP
[14/Sep/2013:16:33:43 -0600] BIND REQ conn=55 op=0 msgID=1 type=SIMPLE
dn="cn=Directory Manager"
[14/Sep/2013:16:33:43 -0600] BIND RES conn=55 op=0 msgID=1 result=0
authDN="cn=Directory Manager,cn=Root DNs,cn=config" etime=0
[14/Sep/2013:16:33:43 -0600] MODIFYDN REQ conn=55 op=1 msgID=2
dn="uid=patron96,ou=patrons,dc=inflinx,dc=com" newRDN="uid=patron96_temp"
deleteOldRDN=true newSuperior="ou=patrons,dc=inflinx,dc=com
[14/Sep/2013:16:33:43 -0600] MODIFYDN RES conn=55 op=1 msgID=2 result=0
etime=1
[14/Sep/2013:16:33:43 -0600] MODIFYDN REQ conn=55 op=2 msgID=3
dn="uid=patron96_temp,ou=patrons,dc=inflinx,dc=com" newRDN="uid=patron96"
deleteOldRDN=true newSuperior="ou=patrons,dc=inflinx,dc=com
[14/Sep/2013:16:33:43 -0600] MODIFYDN RES conn=55 op=2 msgID=3
result=0 etime=0
[14/Sep/2013:16:33:43 -0600] UNBIND REQ conn=55 op=3 msgID=4
[14/Sep/2013:16:33:43 -0600] DISCONNECT conn=55 reason="Client Unbind"
```

For an update operation, as you can guess by now, the Spring LDAP infrastructure calculates compensating ModificationItem list for the modifications that are made on the entry. On a commit, nothing needs to be done. But upon a rollback, the computed compensating ModificationItem list will be written back.

Summary

In this chapter, you explored the basics of transactions and looked at Spring LDAP's transaction support. Spring LDAP keeps a record of the state in the LDAP tree before performing an operation. If a rollback were to happen, Spring LDAP performs compensating operations to restore the previous state. Keep in mind that this compensating transaction support gives an illusion of atomicity but doesn't guarantee it.

In the next chapter, you will explore other Spring LDAP features such as connection pooling and LDIF parsing.

CHAPTER 10

■ ■ ■

Odds and Ends

In this chapter, you will learn

- How to perform authentication using Spring LDAP

- How to parse LDIF files

- LDAP connection pooling

Authentication Using Spring LDAP

Authentication is a common operation performed against LDAP servers. This usually involves verifying a username and password against the information stored in the directory server.

One approach for implementing authentication using Spring LDAP is via the getContext method of the ContextSource class. Here is the getContext method API:

```
DirContext getContext(String  principal, String credentials) throws
NamingException
```

The principal parameter is the fully qualified DN of the user, and the credentials parameter is the user's password. The method uses the passed-in information to authenticate against LDAP. Upon successful authentication, the method returns a DirContext instance representing the user's entry. Authentication failures are communicated to the caller via an exception. Listing 10-1 gives a DAO implementation for authenticating patrons in your Library application using the getContext technique.

Listing 10-1.

```
package com.inflinx.book.ldap.repository;

import javax.naming.directory.DirContext;
import org.springframework.beans.factory.annotation.Autowired;
import org.springframework.beans.factory.annotation.Qualifier;
import org.springframework.ldap.NamingException;
import org.springframework.ldap.core.ContextSource;
import org.springframework.ldap.core.DistinguishedName;
```

```
import org.springframework.ldap.support.LdapUtils;
import org.springframework.stereotype.Repository;

@Repository("authenticationDao")
public class AuthenticationDaoImpl implements AuthenticationDao{

    public static final String BASE_DN = "ou=patrons,dc=inflinx,dc=com";

    @Autowired
    @Qualifier("contextSource")
    private ContextSource contextSource;

    @Override
    public boolean authenticate(String userid, String password) {
        DistinguishedName dn = new DistinguishedName(BASE_DN);
        dn.add("uid", userid);
        DirContext authenticatedContext = null;
        try {
            authenticatedContext = contextSource.getContext( dn.toString(),
            password);
            return true;
        }
        catch(NamingException e) {
            e.printStackTrace();
            return false;
        }
        finally {
            LdapUtils.closeContext(authenticatedContext);
        }
    }
}
```

The getContext method requires a fully qualified DN of the user entry. Hence, the authentication method starts out by creating a DistinguishedName instance with the supplied "ou=patrons,dc=inflinx,dc=com" base. Then you append the provided userid to the DN to create the patron's fully qualified DN. The authentication method then invokes the getContext method, passing in the string representation of the patron's DN and password. A successful authentication simply exits the method with a return value of true. Notice that in the finally block you are closing the obtained context.

Listing 10-2 shows a JUnit test to verify the proper working of this authenticate method.

Listing 10-2.

```
package com.inflinx.book.ldap.parser;

import org.junit.Assert;
import org.junit.Test;
import org.junit.runner.RunWith;
```

```
import org.springframework.beans.factory.annotation.Autowired;
import org.springframework.beans.factory.annotation.Qualifier;
import org.springframework.test.context.ContextConfiguration;
import org.springframework.test.context.junit4.SpringJUnit4ClassRunner;
import com.inflinx.book.ldap.repository.AuthenticationDao;

@RunWith(SpringJUnit4ClassRunner.class)
@ContextConfiguration("classpath:repositoryContext-test.xml")

public class AuthenticationDaoTest {

@Autowired
@Qualifier("authenticationDao")
private AuthenticationDao authenticationDao;

    @Test
    public void testAuthenticate() {
        boolean authResult = authenticationDao.authenticate("patron0",
        "password");
        Assert.assertTrue(authResult);
        authResult = authenticationDao.authenticate("patron0",
        "invalidPassword");
        Assert.assertFalse(authResult);
    }
}
```

The repositoryContext-test.xml associated with Listing 10-2 is shown in Listing 10-3. In this scenario, you are working with your installed OpenDJ LDAP server.

Listing 10-3.

```
<?xml version="1.0" encoding="UTF-8"?>
<beans xmlns="http://www.springframework.org/schema/beans"
xmlns:xsi="http://www.w3.org/2001/XMLSchema-instance"
xmlns:context="http://www.springframework.org/schema/context"
xsi:schemaLocation="http://www.springframework.org/schema/beans
http://www.springframework.org/schema/beans/spring-beans.xsd
http://www.springframework.org/schema/context
http://www.springframework.org/schema/context/spring-context.xsd">

    <context:component-scan base-package="com.inflinx.book.ldap" />

    <bean id="contextSource" class="org.springframework.ldap.core.support.
    LdapContextSource">
        <property name="url" value="ldap://localhost:11389" />
        <property name="userDn" value="cn=Directory Manager" />
        <property name="password" value="opendj" />
        <property name="base" value=""/>
```

175

```
        </bean>
        <bean id="ldapTemplate" class="org.springframework.ldap.core.
        LdapTemplate">
            <constructor-arg ref="contextSource" />
        </bean>
</beans>
```

The only drawback with the implementation shown in Listing 10-3 is that the getContext method requires the fully qualified DN of the patron entry. There could be scenarios where the client's code might not know the fully qualified DN of the user. In Listing 10-1, you append a hard-coded value to create the fully qualified DN. This approach will fail if you want to start using the code in Listing 10-1, say, to authenticate your library's employees also. To address such situations, Spring LDAP added several variations of the authenticate method shown below to the LdapTemplate class:

```
boolean authenticate(String base, String filter,  String password)
```

This authenticate method uses the supplied base DN and filter parameters to perform a search for the user's LDAP entry. If an entry is found, the fully qualified DN of the user is extracted. Then, this DN, along with the password, is passed to the ContextSource's getContext method to perform authentication. Essentially this is a two-step process but it alleviates the need for fully qualified DN upfront. Listing 10-4 contains the modified authentication implementation. Notice that the authenticate method signature in the DAO implementation has not changed. It still accepts the username and password as its parameters. But thanks to the authenticate method abstraction, the implementation has become lot simpler. The implementation passes an empty base DN since you want the search to be performed relative to the base DN used during ContextSource creation.

Listing 10-4.

```
package com.inflinx.book.ldap.repository;

import org.springframework.beans.factory.annotation.Autowired;
import org.springframework.beans.factory.annotation.Qualifier;
import org.springframework.ldap.core.LdapTemplate;
import org.springframework.stereotype.Repository;

@Repository("authenticationDao2")
public class AuthenticationDaoImpl2 implements AuthenticationDao {

    @Autowired
    @Qualifier("ldapTemplate")
    private LdapTemplate ldapTemplate;

    @Override
    public boolean authenticate(String userid, String password){
        return ldapTemplate.authenticate("","(uid=" + userid + ")", password);
    }
}
```

Listing 10-5 shows the JUnit test case to verify the above authenticate method implementation.

Listing 10-5.

```
package com.inflinx.book.ldap.parser;

import org.junit.Assert;
import org.junit.Test;
import org.junit.runner.RunWith;
import org.springframework.beans.factory.annotation.Autowired;
import org.springframework.beans.factory.annotation.Qualifier;
import org.springframework.test.context.ContextConfiguration;
import org.springframework.test.context.junit4.SpringJUnit4ClassRunner;
import com.inflinx.book.ldap.repository.AuthenticationDao;

@RunWith(SpringJUnit4ClassRunner.class)
@ContextConfiguration("classpath:repositoryContext-test.xml")
public class AuthenticationDao2Test {

@Autowired
@Qualifier("authenticationDao2")
private AuthenticationDao authenticationDao;

    @Test
    public void testAuthenticate() {
        boolean authResult = authenticationDao.authenticate("patron0", "password");
        Assert.assertTrue(authResult);
        authResult = authenticationDao.authenticate("patron0","invalidPassword");
        Assert.assertFalse(authResult);
    }
}
```

Handling Authentication Exceptions

The previous authenticate methods in LdapTemplate simply tell you whether authentication succeeded or failed. There will be cases where you are interested in the actual exception that caused the failure. For those scenarios, LdapTemplate provides overloaded versions of the authenticate method. The API for one of the overloaded authenticate methods is as follows:

```
boolean authenticate(String base, String filter,  String  password,
AuthenticationErrorCallback errorCallback);
```

Any exceptions that occur during the execution of the above authenticate method will be passed on to an AuthenticationErrorCallback instance provided as the method parameter. This collected exception can be logged or used for post-authentication processes. Listing 10-6 and Listing 10-7 show the AuthenticationErrorCallback API and its simple implementation, respectively. The execute method in the callback can decide what to do with the raised exception. In your simple implementation, you are just storing it and making it available to the LdapTemplate's search caller.

Listing 10-6.

```
package org.springframework.ldap.core;

public interface AuthenticationErrorCallback {
    public void execute(Exception e);
}
```

Listing 10-7.

```
package com.practicalspring.ldap.repository;

import org.springframework.ldap.core.AuthenticationErrorCallback;

public class EmployeeAuthenticationErrorCallback implements
AuthenticationErrorCallback {

    private Exception authenticationException;

    @Override
    public void execute(Exception e) {
        this.authenticationException = e;
    }

    public Exception getAuthenticationException() {
        return authenticationException;
    }
}
```

Listing 10-8 shows the modified AuthenticationDao implementation along with the error callback; here you are simply logging the failed exception to the console. Listing 10-9 shows the JUnit test.

Listing 10-8.

```
package com.practicalspring.ldap.repository;

import org.springframework.beans.factory.annotation.Autowired;
import org.springframework.beans.factory.annotation.Qualifier;
import org.springframework.ldap.core.LdapTemplate;
import org.springframework.stereotype.Repository;
```

```
@Repository("authenticationDao3")
public class AuthenticationDaoImpl3 implements AuthenticationDao {

@Autowired
@Qualifier("ldapTemplate")
private LdapTemplate ldapTemplate;

    @Override
    public boolean authenticate(String userid, String password){
        EmployeeAuthenticationErrorCallback errorCallback = new
        EmployeeAuthenticationErrorCallback();
        boolean isAuthenticated = ldapTemplate.authenticate("","(uid=" +
        userid + ")", password, errorCallback);
        if(!isAuthenticated) {
            System.out.println(errorCallback.getAuthenticationException());
        }
        return isAuthenticated;
    }
}
```

Listing 10-9.

```
package com.inflinx.book.ldap.parser;

import org.junit.Assert;
import org.junit.Test;
import org.junit.runner.RunWith;
import org.springframework.beans.factory.annotation.Autowired;
import org.springframework.beans.factory.annotation.Qualifier;
import org.springframework.test.context.ContextConfiguration;
import org.springframework.test.context.junit4.SpringJUnit4ClassRunner;
import com.inflinx.book.ldap.repository.AuthenticationDao;

@RunWith(SpringJUnit4ClassRunner.class)
@ContextConfiguration("classpath:repositoryContext-test.xml")
public class AuthenticationDao3Test {

@Autowired
@Qualifier("authenticationDao3")
private AuthenticationDao authenticationDao;

    @Test
    public void testAuthenticate() {
        boolean authResult = authenticationDao.authenticate("patron0",
        "invalidPassword");
        Assert.assertFalse(authResult);
    }
}
```

Upon running the JUnit test in Listing 10-9, you should see the following error message in the console:

```
org.springframework.ldap.AuthenticationException: [LDAP:
error code 49 - Invalid Credentials]; nested exception is
javax.naming.AuthenticationException: [LDAP: error code 49 -
Invalid Credentials]
```

Parsing LDIF Data

The LDAP Data Interchange Format is a standards-based data interchange format for representing LDAP directory data in a flat file format. LDIF is discussed in detail in Chapter 1. As an LDAP developer or administrator, you may sometimes need to parse LDIF files and perform operations such as a bulk directory load. For such scenarios, Spring LDAP introduced a set of classes in the org.springframework.ldap.ldif package and its subpackages that make it easy to read and parse LDIF files.

Central to the org.springframework.ldap.ldif.parser package is the Parser interface and its default implementation LdifParser. The LdifParser is responsible for reading individual lines from an LDIF file and converting them into Java objects. This object representation is possible through two newly added classes, namely LdapAttribute and LdapAttributes.

The code in Listing 10-10 uses LdifParser to read and print the total number of records in an LDIF file. You start the implementation by creating an instance of LdifParser and passing in the file you would like to parse. Before the parser can be used, you need to open it. Then you use the parser's iterator style interface for reading and counting individual records.

Listing 10-10.

```
package com.inflinx.book.ldap.parser;

import java.io.File;
import java.io.IOException;
import org.springframework.core.io.ClassPathResource;
import org.springframework.ldap.core.LdapAttributes;
import org.springframework.ldap.ldif.parser.LdifParser;

public class SimpleLdifParser {

    public void parse(File file) throws IOException {
        LdifParser parser = new LdifParser(file);
        parser.open();
        int count = 0;
        while(parser.hasMoreRecords()) {
            LdapAttributes attributes = parser.getRecord();
            count ++;
        }
```

```
        parser.close();
        System.out.println(count);
    }

    public static void main(String[] args) throws IOException {
        SimpleLdifParser parser = new SimpleLdifParser();
        parser.parse(new ClassPathResource("patrons.ldif").getFile());
    }
}
```

Before running the above class, make sure that you have the patrons.ldif file in the classpath. Upon running the class with the patrons.ldif file included with the Chapter 10 code, you should see the count 103 printed to the console.

The parsing implementation of LdifParser relies on three supporting policy definitions: separator policy, attribute validation policy, and record specification policy.

- The separator policy provides the separation rules for LDIF records in a file and is defined in the RFC 2849. It is implemented via the org.springframework.ldap.ldif.support. SeparatorPolicy class.

- The attribute validation policy, as the name suggests, is used to ensure that all the attributes are structured properly in the LDIF file prior to parsing. It is implemented via the AttributeValidationPolicy interface and the DefaultAttributeValidationPolicy class. These two are located in the org.springframework.ldap.ldif.support package. The DefaultAttributeValidationPolicy uses regular expressions to validate attribute format according to RFC 2849.

- The record specification policy is used to validate rules that each LDIF record must confirm to. Spring LDAP provides the Specification interface and two implementations for this policy: org.springframework. ldap.schema.DefaultSchemaSpecification and org. springframework.ldap.schema.BasicSchemaSpecification. The DefaultSchemaSpecification has an empty implementation and does not really validate the records. The BasicSchemaSpecification can be used to perform basic checks such as that an objectClass must exist for each LAP entry. For most cases, the BasicSchemaSpecification will suffice.

The modified parse method implementation, along with the three policy definitions, is given in Listing 10-11.

Listing 10-11.

```
package com.inflinx.book.ldap.parser;

import java.io.File;
import java.io.IOException;
import org.springframework.core.io.ClassPathResource;
import org.springframework.ldap.core.LdapAttributes;
import org.springframework.ldap.ldif.parser.LdifParser;
import org.springframework.ldap.ldif.support.DefaultAttributeValidationPolicy;
import org.springframework.ldap.schema.BasicSchemaSpecification;

public class SimpleLdifParser2 {

    public void parse(File file) throws IOException {
        LdifParser parser = new LdifParser(file);
        parser.setAttributeValidationPolicy(new DefaultAttributeValidationPolicy());
        parser.setRecordSpecification(new BasicSchemaSpecification());
        parser.open();
            int count = 0;
        while(parser.hasMoreRecords()) {
            LdapAttributes attributes = parser.getRecord();
            count ++;
        }
        parser.close();
        System.out.println(count);
    }

    public static void main(String[] args) throws IOException {
        SimpleLdifParser2 parser = new SimpleLdifParser2();
        parser.parse(new ClassPathResource("patrons.ldif").getFile());
    }
}
```

Upon running the above method, you should see the count 103 in the console.

LDAP Connection Pooling

LDAP connection pooling is a technique where connections to LDAP directory are reused rather than being created each time a connection is requested. Without connection pooling, each request to LDAP directory causes a new connection to be created and then released when the connection is no longer required. Creating a new connection is resource-intensive and this overhead can have adverse effects on performance. With connection pooling, connections are stored in pool after they are created and are recycled for subsequent client requests.

Connections in a pool at any point can be in one of these three states:

- **In Use:** The connection is open and currently in use.

- **Idle:** The connection is open and available for reuse.

- **Closed:** The connection is no longer available for use.

Figure 10-1 illustrates the possible actions on a connection at any given time.

Figure 10-1. *Connection pool states*

Built In Connection Pooling

JNDI provides basic support for connection pooling via the `"com.sun.jndi.ldap.connect.pool"` environment property. Applications creating a directory context can set this property to true and indicate that connection pooling needs to be turned on. Listing 10-12 shows the plain JNDI code that utilizes pooling support.

Listing 10-12.

```
// Set up environment for creating initial context
Hashtable env = new Hashtable();
env.put(Context.INITIAL_CONTEXT_FACTORY, "com.sun.jndi.ldap.
LdapCtxFactory");
env.put(Context.PROVIDER_URL, "ldap://localhost:11389");

// Enable connection pooling
env.put("com.sun.jndi.ldap.connect.pool", "true");

// Create one initial context
(Get connection from pool) DirContext ctx = new InitialDirContext(env);

// do something useful with ctx
// Close the context when we're done
ctx.close(); // Return connection to pool
```

By default the contexts created using Spring LDAP have the `"com.sun.jndi.ldap.connect.pool"` property set to `false`. The native connection pooling can be turned on by setting the pooled property of the `LdapContextSource` to `true` in the configuration file. The following code shows the configuration change:

```
<bean id="contextSource" class="org.springframework.ldap.core.support.
LdapContextSource">
    <property name="url" value="ldap://localhost:11389" />
```

```
    <property name="base" value="dc=example,dc=com" />
    <property name="userDn" value="cn=Manager" />
    <property name="password" value="secret" />
    <property name="pooled" value="true"/>
</bean>
```

Though the native LDAP connection pooling is simple, it does suffer from certain drawbacks. The pool of connections is maintained per the Java Runtime Environment. It is not possible to maintain multiple connection pools per JVM. Also, there is no control over the properties of the connection pool, such as the number of connections to be maintained at any time or idle connection time. It is also not possible to provide any custom connection validation to ensure that pooled connections are still valid.

Spring LDAP Connection Pooling

In order to address shortcomings with native JNDI pooling, Spring LDAP provides a custom pooling library for LDAP connections. The Spring LDAP pooling library maintains its own set of LDAP connections that are specific to each application.

■ **Note** Spring LDAP utilizes the Jakarta Commons Pool library for its underlying pooling implementation.

Central to Spring LDAP pooling is the org.springframework.ldap.pool. factory.PoolingContextSource, which is a specialized ContextSource implementation and is responsible for pooling DirContext instances. To utilize connection pooling, you start by configuring a Spring LDAP Context Source, as shown:

```
<bean id="contextSourceTarget" class="org.springframework.ldap.core.support.
LdapContextSource">
    <property name="url" value="ldap://localhost:389" />
    <property name="base" value="dc=example,dc=com" />
    <property name="userDn" value="cn=Manager" />
    <property name="password" value="secret" />
    <property name="pooled" value="false"/>
</bean>
```

Note that you have the pooled property of the context source set to false. This will allow the LdapContextSource create brand new connections when the need arises. Also, the id of the ContextSource is now set to contextSourceTarget instead of contextSource, which is what you usually use. The next step is to create a PoolingContextSource, as shown:

```
<bean id="contextSource" class="org.springframework.ldap.pool.factory.
PoolingContextSource">
    <property name="contextSource" ref="contextSourceTarget" />
</bean>
```

The PoolingContextSource wraps the contextSourceTarget you configured earlier. This is required since the PoolingContextSource delegates the actual creation of DirContexts to the contextSourceTarget. Also note that you have used the id contextSource for this bean instance. This allows you to keep the configuration changes to minimum while using a PoolingContextSource instance in an LdapTemplate, as shown:

```
<bean id="ldapTemplate" class="org.springframework.ldap.core.LdapTemplate">
  <constructor-arg ref="contextSource" />
</bean>
```

The PoolingContextSource provides a variety of options that can be used to fine-tune connection pooling. Table 10-1 lists some of the important configuration properties.

Table 10-1. *PoolingContextSource Configuration Properties*

Property	Description	Default
testOnBorrow	When set to true, the DirContext is validated before it is borrowed from the pool. If the DirContext fails validation, it is removed from the pool and a new attempt is made to borrow another DirContext. This testing might add a small delay in serving the borrow request.	False
testOnReturn	When set to true, this property indicates that DirContext will be validated before returning to the pool.	False
testWhileIdle	When set to true, this property indicates that idle DirContext instances in the pool should be validated at a specified frequency. Objects failing the validation will be dropped from the pool.	False
timeBetweenEvictionRunsMillis	This property indicates the time in milliseconds to sleep between running idle context tests. A negative number indicates that idle test will never be run.	-1
whenExhaustedAction	Specifies the action to be taken when the pool is exhausted. The possible options are WHEN_EXHAUSTED_FAIL (0), WHEN_EXHAUSTED_BLOCK (1), and WHEN_EXHAUSTED_GROW (2).	1
maxTotal	The maximum number of active connections that this pool can contain. A non-positive integer indicates no limit.	-1

(*continued*)

Table 10-1. (*continued*)

Property	Description	Default
maxIdle	The maximum number of idle connections of each type (read, read-write) that can be idle in the pool.	8
maxWait	The maximum number of milliseconds that a pool will wait for a connection to be returned to the pool before throwing an exception. A negative number indicates indefinite wait.	-1

Pool Validation

Spring LDAP makes it easy to validate pooled connections. This validation ensures that the DirContext instances are properly configured and connected to LDAP server before they are borrowed from the pool. The same validation is done before the contexts are returned to the pool or on the contexts sitting idle in the pool.

The PoolingContextSource delegates the actual validation to concrete instances of the org.springframework.ldap.pool.validation.DirContextValidator interface. In Listing 10-13 you can see that the DirContextValidator has only one method: validateDirContext. The first parameter, contextType, indicates if the context to be validated is a read-only or a read-write context. The second parameter is the actual context that needs to be validated.

Listing 10-13.

```
package org.springframework.ldap.pool.validation;

import javax.naming.directory.DirContext;
import org.springframework.ldap.core.ContextSource;
import org.springframework.ldap.pool.DirContextType;

public interface DirContextValidator {
    boolean validateDirContext(DirContextType contextType, DirContext dirContext);
}
```

Out of the box, Spring LDAP provides an aptly named default implementation of the DirContextValidator called org.springframework.ldap.pool.validation. DefaultDirContextValidator. This implementation simply performs a search using the context and verifies the returned javax.naming.NamingEnumeration. If the NamingEnumeration does not contain any results or if an exception is thrown, the context fails the validation and will be removed from the pool. Applications requiring more sophisticated validation can create new implementations of the DirContextValidator interface.

Configuring pooling validation is shown in Listing 10-14. You start by creating a dirContextValidator bean of type DefaultDirContextValidator. Then you modify the contextSource bean declaration to include the dirContextValidator bean. In Listing 10-14, you have also added the testOnBorrow and testWhileIdle properties.

Listing 10-14.

```
<bean id="dirContextValidator" class="org.springframework.ldap.pool.
validation.DefaultDirContextValidator" />
<bean id="contextSource" class="org.springframework.ldap.pool.factory.
PoolingContextSource">
    <property name="contextSource" ref="contextSourceTarget" />
    <property name="dirContextValidator" ref="dirContextValidator"/>
    <property name="testOnBorrow" value="true" />
    <property name="testWhileIdle" value="true" />
</bean>
```

Summary

This brings us to the end of our journey. Throughout the book, you have learned the key features of Spring LDAP. With this knowledge, you should be ready to start developing Spring LDAP-based applications.

Finally, it has been an absolute pleasure writing this book and sharing my insights with you. I wish you all the best. Happy coding!

Index

■ V, W, X, Y, Z

Get the eBook for only $10!

Now you can take the weightless companion with you anywhere, anytime. Your purchase of this book entitles you to 3 electronic versions for only $10.

This Apress title will prove so indispensible that you'll want to carry it with you everywhere, which is why we are offering the eBook in 3 formats for only $10 if you have already purchased the print book.

Convenient and fully searchable, the PDF version enables you to easily find and copy code—or perform examples by quickly toggling between instructions and applications. The MOBI format is ideal for your Kindle, while the ePUB can be utilized on a variety of mobile devices.

Go to www.apress.com/promo/tendollars to purchase your companion eBook.

Apress®
THE EXPERT'S VOICE™

All Apress eBooks are subject to copyright. All rights are reserved by the Publisher, whether the whole or part of the material is concerned, specifically the rights of translation, reprinting, reuse of illustrations, recitation, broadcasting, reproduction on microfilms or in any other physical way, and transmission or information storage and retrieval, electronic adaptation, computer software, or by similar or dissimilar methodology now known or hereafter developed. Exempted from this legal reservation are brief excerpts in connection with reviews or scholarly analysis or material supplied specifically for the purpose of being entered and executed on a computer system, for exclusive use by the purchaser of the work. Duplication of this publication or parts thereof is permitted only under the provisions of the Copyright Law of the Publisher's location, in its current version, and permission for use must always be obtained from Springer. Permissions for use may be obtained through RightsLink at the Copyright Clearance Center. Violations are liable to prosecution under the respective Copyright Law.